How Come We're Alive?

How Come
We're Alive?

CURTIS JONES

WORD BOOKS, Publisher
Waco, Texas

to

Sybil

Nellie

and

Mildred

Contents

Acknowledgments

As in life, the gestation period of a book is a happy, anxious, mutually shared expectancy. Desired results cannot be accelerated. Books, like babies, must grow. It is also a time of joyous hope, fervent prayer, and hard work.

The emergence of this book has been sobering because it deals with life's inevitables. It has afforded me an opportunity to review in considerable depth certain aspects of my ministry.

A number of friends and associates have made possible the production of this volume. I am particularly indebted to Floyd W. Thatcher, vice-president and executive editor, Word Books, Publisher, Waco, Texas, for planting the seed; Marvin G. Osborn, Jr., financial consultant, St. Louis, Missouri, and James S. Duncan, School of Journalism, Drake University, Des Moines, Iowa, for critical readings of the manuscript; Jack V. Reeves, regional minister of the Christian Church in Illinois, for substantiating the John F. M. Parker story and permission to use it; George W. Sullivan, Des Moines, Iowa, and Ronald T. Knight, Macon, Georgia, attorneys, for considerable assistance with the legal glossary; Guy Brown, pastor, Christ Lutheran Church, San Angelo, Texas, for helpful conversations during the embryonic stage.

As in every endeavor, I am grateful to Sybil for her encouragement, inspiration, and inciteful criticisms.

Simultaneously I wish to acknowledge the contributions of my secretary, Mrs. Charles L. Patrick, in producing the typescript.

CURTIS JONES

Prologue

When Titus Flavius Vespasianus, emperor of Rome, A.D. 70–79, left the city to finish his days in the country, he is said to have remarked: "I have passed sixty and ten years upon the earth and I have lived seven of them."

How many years, days, have you actually lived? Yesterday, for instance, did you live or merely oscillate between options and hope? Today?

Life is irreversible. There are no instant replays in the drama of living. The real diary of our days is written, not in rhetoric, intentions, or promotions, but in the manner in which we receive and share life. We are constantly reminded of its illusiveness and brevity, harshness and beauty.

The miracle of being alive was radiantly apparent on the faces of POWs returning from Vietnam. Tedious days followed by long, lonely nights, humiliation, and apprehension failed to crush their spirits or distort their purpose. Their return did more for America than America ever did for them. To view their ecstasy was to ask, How come I'm alive? My peers are dying off. Some are maimed, diseased and lonely, pain their constant companion.

Reflecting on forty years in the ministry, I find my faith in the eternal now, the Christian life, substantiated by stalwarts I have known and buried. I have seen prominent businessmen, stripped of their fortunes, humbly adjust to different life-styles; mothers accept with grace the pregnancy of unmarried daughters; children struck by incurable diseases die without fear; students flunk out of college and discipline themselves to try again; a parent holding the family together after the disappearance of a mate. I have witnessed death and life—from homicide to suicide, from stillbirth to senility, from arrogance to sainthood. Although at times life may appear repulsive, it can be beautiful, purposeful, contagious, redemptive.

As Henry Wadsworth Longfellow lay in state, his friend of many years, Ralph Waldo Emerson, whose memory was failing, came to pay his respects. Asked if he could identify the deceased, he thoughtfully replied, "I don't remember this gentleman's name, but he was a white soul."

How inadequate Emerson's declaration when we come to the death of Jesus. Who can fully comprehend the cross? Who can articulate the abiding message of the atonement? Perhaps no one; yet we understand sufficiently the mystery to know that through the mighty acts of God life has been given direction, depth, dignity, and indestructibility.

Three men were crucified on Good Friday. Those occupying the outer crosses were killed because their conduct was below accepted standards; the man on the center cross was executed because his standards were too high. The mob could see no difference. One is reminded of the comment of George Bernard Shaw who, upon hearing of the assassination of Gandhi, quipped: "It is dangerous to be too good."

And so it is! This is the paradox of life. If you are too bad, you will get in trouble; if you are too good, you will have difficulty. What then is one to do? Compromise for security? No! The choice is courage.

The challenge of living is to find God's continuing will

for our lives. As we experience growth and truth, it becomes incumbent upon us to pursue our work with diligence and devotion.

I hope this book may aid in the perennial search for the meaning and stewardship of living; that we may glimpse the grace necessary to cope with and conquer our inadequacies, fears, and tribulations; coming at last to face death with the confidence and hope demonstrated by Jesus when he said: "Father! In your hands I place my spirit" (Luke 23:46, TEV).

1

How Come We're Still Alive?

Life is but a day at most.
Robert Burns

Christianity is not one ideology over
against other ideologies. It is a life
inspired by the Holy Spirit.
Paul Tournier

Man is too grand to waste, even though
he is too miserable to save himself.
Elton Trueblood

I have come that men may have life, and
may have it in all its fullness.
Jesus, John 10:10, NEB

Among the heroes of World War II are survivors from
the First, Third, and Fourth Ranger Battalions, an outfit
dating back to June, 1942. The Rangers spearheaded every
major American thrust in the Mediterranean theater and
were exposed to as much danger as any United States in-
fantrymen. Losses among the original Rangers were as-

13

tonishingly high. Out of the 1,500 men who composed the three battalions, only 199 survived, 64 of whom received the Purple Heart.

Following the war when Rangers met, they did not exchange the usual "Hello" or "I am glad to see you," but "How come we're still alive?" Their postwar greeting is more than a report of stamina and sacrifice. It is a continuing, inescapable drama: Why are you alive? What are you doing to register gratitude, to help others find fulfillment? You who have experienced a minimum of loneliness, suffering, and pain, what are you doing with your life?

Man's determination to live is inconceivable. His resiliency and his ability to assimilate pain, suffering, and fear are beyond description.

A Uruguayan plane crashed in the snow-capped Andes of South America in mid-October, 1972. There were forty-five aboard; sixteen survived. These stranded, isolated souls battled for life in sub-zero temperature for seventy-three days. With the minimum of everything except courage, they struggled to outwit death. The survivors were men, and all but one was under twenty-six years of age. Some were rugby players in excellent condition.

These lonely, hungry, cold passengers became so desperate they resorted to cannibalism. One of the group said, "It was like a heart transplant, the dead sustained the living."

At last, two from the heroic band climbed down the mountain in search of help. Ten days later they returned via helicopter with rescue workers.

On January 2, 1968, Professor Christiaan Barnard and a team of fifty-one men and women performed a successful heart transplant. The patient, Dr. Philip Blaiberg, was a dentist from Capetown, South Africa. The world waited in hope and prayer as the heart of Clive Haup, a black man who had met with an accident while vacationing at Glencairn Beach, was transferred from his body to Dr. Blaiberg's. Finally the long operation was completed. After being unconscious for five days, the patient's first words were, "I'm alive. I can breathe now without difficulty or coughing."

For seventy-four days, he lived in a sterile suite. One night Dr. Barnard, wearing his usual hospital garb, walked into the patient's room carrying a transparent plastic box. With cool, professional concern, Professor Barnard said to Dr. Blaiberg, "Do you realize that you are the first man, in the history of mankind, to be able to sit, as you are now, and look at his own dead heart?"

On March 16 Philip Blaiberg was discharged from the hospital. Amid joyful banter and reckless nostalgia, Dr. Barnard said, "Dr. Blaiberg is passing into a bacteria-filled world." Waiting to be escorted home, the famous patient wondered how fresh air, rays of the sun on his face, and the caress of wind would feel. He was alive!

Back of phenomenal experiments in the re-creation of life, despite fantastic accomplishments of technology, remains the haunting question, What is life?

Two philosophical approaches dominate—the naturalistic and the idealistic. The naturalistic philosopher maintains that the scientific method is the only true approach to knowledge. Moreover, he asserts that the real world is the one that can be measured and defined by natural sciences. From this point of view, man is little more than crawling carbohydrates.

The idealistic philosopher avoids the inconsistencies and incompleteness of naturalistic thinking by pointing to the ideas and ideals of man. To him these are the real keys to understanding life. Georg Wilhelm Friedrich Hegel said, "Life is a system of meaning, and the real is the rational and the rational is real." Immanuel Kant maintained, "Life is an endless process toward moral perfection."

Much is being said today about a philosophy known as existentialism—experiencing and defining life in practical terms. One who accepts this concept can never be an impartial observer; his own existence is at stake! He does not look for a complete answer to the meaning of life but, in the words of Paul Tillich, prays for "the courage to continue." Time is irreplaceable, irreversible; the now is all-important. The real mystery to the existentialist is his own existence!

In *How Are You Programmed?* J. Edward Barrett refers to man as the "presiding self." How do you think of him? Is man just an animal who remembers, who takes out insurance and becomes obese with age? Is he a monkey capable of doing mathematics?

Lesser animals seem to be genetically and historically programmed, their behavior determined. The activity of a spider, for instance, is predetermined. While that of a dog is less restricted, his world is indeed limited.

Although man has more in common with the animal kingdom than he cares to admit, he is nonetheless capable of presiding over both his genetic and his historic programming. He is free to choose courses of action, to commit himself to objectives; he is intimately related to the living cosmos. He can control the life cycle of fellow creatures and of himself.

Man's uninhibited freedom enables him to be self-critical, a distinguishing characteristic of the human race. His freedom also finds expression in hope, an orientation toward a better future where values and conditions are yet to be attained. The presiding man has capacity to create. He has built-in controls and the ability to absorb injury and transform it into strength.

Jesus was a victim of prejudice and polarization. He called men into a relationship, a reign of goodwill and compassion referred to as the kingdom of God. They responded with a cross! Yet the Lord so absorbed his hurt—man's maliciousness—that the cross became a symbol of suffering love, salvation.

No other animal plants flowers or builds cities, churches, and highways. Only man composes symphonies. Only man reduces the indigenous harmonies of the universe into discord, division, and war. Only man may succeed in committing suicide by orgy. Man alone has the capacity to experience awe and to worship.

Although resembling God, man abuses his freedom. Destructive consequences follow, not from genetic or historic programming, but from the freedom of presiding self. As Dr. Barrett says, "Sin is fundamentally a refusal to be self-critical."

The Greeks interpreted life in terms of tragedy; Hebrews, guilt. The New Testament focuses on a man sent by God. He lived, absorbing abuse and symbolizing concern. He was so committed to the presiding Father that nothing frightened him, not even death. The Nazarene actualized among men their common greeting—*Shalom!*

Science and philosophy start exploring the rational life with man. Arthur Koestler refers to scientists as "Peeping

Toms at the keyhole of eternity." Christian theology begins with the loving Father. The Bible opens with the words, "In the beginning God created the heavens and the earth" (Gen. 1:1, RSV). Later in the narration we read, "Let us make man in our image, after our likeness. . . . So God created . . . them" (Gen. 1:26–27, RSV). Near the close of the biblical account is this assurance: "I am the Alpha and the Omega, the first and the last, the beginning and the end" (Rev. 22:13, RSV). God is life; life is God.

Those who accept Christ as the visible likeness of God see life as interrelated and understand it in terms of creation, history, and hope. The Christian believes God offers new life through his Son who declared his mission was to bequeath it. This assurance includes, not only the abundance of things, but vision to see new horizons, spaciousness of spirit, and dimensions and depths of understanding.

Ask the average churchgoer what life is all about, and he is apt to concede that it's puzzling but seems to be divided into two parts: good and evil, body and soul. This dualism has persisted for centuries. The Greeks made much of it. But the Bible teaches that man is a psychological and spiritual whole and that the value and destiny of life is not determined by things or philosophies but by one's relationship to Almighty God!

To some it would seem that life is just a physical escalation from inception, to birth, to death, with the normal stresses peculiar to each period of development. Others leave the impression that existence is synonymous with the ownership and use of physical property—if not people.

Affluent Americans have the reputation for loving things and using people. But is life simply a matter of debits and

18

credits, mortgages, titles of ownership? Is life just paying bills, maintaining schedules, breathing? Is it just what we term success, sex?

Many place high priority on social and racial superiority. Those at the top of the pyramid feel more secure when walking on the shoulders and living from the labors of those beneath. Life to them is position, advantage, power.

The tycoon views life in terms of power. It may be political, economic, social, or religious, but however it appears, the aim is the same—control! When an individual or a company gives sizeable amounts to elect one to political office, it is well to remember these are not gifts, but investments which donors hope will produce additional prestige and profits.

Economic man, unique to twentieth-century technological progress, is frequently oblivious to life's interdependencies outside his own milieu. Reduced, if not controlled, by an ever-expanding Gross National Product, he is always on the edge of replacement and destruction. The system breeds animosity.

Economic man continues to search for higher offers, not necessarily higher motives. Frequently he is immune to social and religious stimuli. Conditioned by the hire-fire cycle—which keeps wage-costs, production, consumer enthusiasms in delicate balance—he is forever pressing for shorter hours, better working conditions, benefits, and more money. He is never satisfied, for his motives are inadequate.

In *Corporation Man*, British TV producer and management consultant, Antony Jay, sees the modern business executive as a hunter who, like his ancient predecessor, leaves the tribe each day to stalk, capture, and return to camp with his prey. To him business is directed more from primitive instincts of tribal survival than logical rationale.

To be sure, man is more than a hunter! He can read and write, compose music, build computers, adapt to space, and walk on the moon. These are additions, not subtractions, from the hunter instinct.

A "new biology" is emerging. The fascination is not so much new facts, data processing, but new ways of looking at problems, the world, one's colleagues, self, life! Antony Jay calls it "the acceptance of the irrational."

Each of us sees life differently. Shakespeare's Macbeth declared:

> Life's but a walking shadow, a poor player
> That struts and frets his hour upon the stage,
> And then is heard no more; it is a tale
> Told by an idiot, full of sound and fury,
> Signifying nothing.

To some, life is "a walking shadow," a statistic, a race with death, but in more rational moments they revere it as the precious gift of God. No one asked to be born, and relatively few ask to die. The miracle of life is more mysterious than the miracle of death.

Giants of history leave the impression they were in tune with life and met it with grace, courage, joy, and commitment. In her biography of Oliver Wendell Holmes, Catherine Bowen declared that the secret of the judge's success was "his manner of meeting life." Similar characteristics were observed in the life-styles of presidents Harry S. Truman and Lyndon B. Johnson.

How Come We're Still Alive?

If contagious aliveness is discernible in attitude and action, how are we to meet life? This is the art we seek in a complex and demanding society. It is difficult to overcome cynicism, distrust, and harsh criticism when subterfuge, politics, and corruption are rampant.

At the news of the death of Matthew Arnold, a neighbor observed, "Poor Matthew, he won't like God." This is the prevailing mood! So often it is not a matter of coping with life, but enduring it; it seems so hopeless, unfair, and painful that we are ready to sign off, irrespective of age, color, or situation.

Some insist on meeting life legalistically. They literally practice the dictum of "an eye for an eye and a tooth for a tooth." The inconceivable intrusion of Arab guerrillas during the 1972 Olympic Games in Munich is a stark reminder of the feuding and senseless killing between Arabs and Jews for centuries. More than retaliation, however, the Arabs seized the moment and the forum to reiterate injustices perpetrated in the Arab-Israeli War of 1948. Life to these nomads is dismal.

There are those who insist on using life as protocol, as a rod to impress or to penalize another. Some parents are compelled to punish. An angry couple in Arizona determined to make a point with their lovely daughter who returned late from a party. The uptight parents handed her a loaded gun and demanded that she kill her pet. Instead she took her life.

Some, of course, lack the perspective, ability, or courage to look life squarely in the face. Consequently they wear many masks and play many games; they seek escape and temporary satisfaction through marijuana haze, pills, drink, and promiscuous sex. It is exceedingly difficult to accept one's own weaknesses.

The brilliant Samuel Johnson once asked a minister to articulate his defects so that he might correct them. To his surprise, the preacher told him he had a hasty temper and was dogmatic. Whereupon Johnson angrily exclaimed, "What? You are a fool! If there is anything I am free from it is a dogmatic, hasty temper; get out of my sight, Sir!"

Few can take the truth. We prefer ambiguous phrases, complimentary adjectives, and discreet finesse which permit us to hold on to our prejudices and our ideas of importance. Transactional behavior becomes more complicated and life counterproductive. This is helpfully delineated in the provocative book, *I'm OK—You're OK*. Writing from a background of twenty-five years in medicine and counseling, Dr. Thomas A. Harris deals with the concept of Transactional Analysis in understandable terms.

Man is the most complicated and magnificent of God's creatures. Conflicts between good and evil have always plagued him. Moses saw goodness as justice; Plato, as wisdom; Jesus, as love. Yet all agree that virtue, however defined, is constantly under attack by something in human nature that is at war with something else.

There are twelve billion cells in the human brain. It records and stores past events as well as the feelings that accompanied those experiences. Human behavior is largely determined by playbacks of previous encounters.

Transactional Analysis recognizes three elements in each person's make-up—Parent, Adult, and Child. The term *Parent* personifies a huge collection of recordings implanted in childhood—mostly don't's and some do's—and accepted as gospel. The Child represents spontaneous emotion, action. Both Parent and Child must engage the Adult, the reality computer. This inner action is powerful, and accordingly there are four possible life positions:

I'm not OK—You're OK

I'm not OK—You're not OK

I'm OK—You're not OK

I'm OK—You're OK

These attitudes reflect the delicate balance, the psychological ticking, that goes on in an individual. Hopefully such an analysis will lead one to a more open, self-accepting, self-permitting, I'm OK—You're OK emotional stance.

Confession without change, however, is a game. From one point of view, Christianity is a new life-style based on I'm OK—You're OK. If the Christian faith were a mere intellectual postulate, it would have died centuries ago. Faith contains the dynamics of change! The Bible presents a gallery of individuals whose lives were transformed by the awareness of God, by the presence and power of Christ.

When one recognizes the miracle of life, its infinite worth, indestructibility, people and priorities become significant. All persons are important, bound together in universal relatedness and love, a relationship which transcends personal existence.

Ralph Waldo Emerson was correct in asserting, "Man is what he thinks about all day long." That which he feeds on, the context in which he finds himself, the playbacks from previous contacts have a frightening and sometimes wonderful way of shaping and strengthening life.

Certainly there is more to existence than experiencing

biological needs and satisfactions; it is more than early retirement, financial security, and companionship. H. G. Wells sensed the challenge of living when he declared that a gentleman is one who puts more into life than he takes out. What a viable test! To be alive is to be involved with mankind.

There is a retired physician, pioneer in radiology, in his eighties, surprisingly strong. When last visiting him, I commented on the grip in his hand. With a twinkle in his eye, he said, "I am not dead yet! I go to the hospital at least once or twice a week to help read x-ray film."

Consider a brilliant editor in retirement. As would be expected, his eyes are failing, but his love for literature and reading is as keen as ever. Weekly he makes the rounds at a geriatric center distributing books.

A young man fresh out of a prestigious university, bulging with idealism and burdened with brotherhood, teaches in a high school and coaches athletics. Seventy to eighty percent of his students are black—disadvantaged, undisciplined, and unloved. His compassion for blacks is increasing; his suspicion of whites is mounting. Life to this neophyte teacher is more than a job, a sports car, and social safaris. It is sharing—at considerable sacrifice—with those in need.

Another gentleman who knows the meaning of life is in his fifties. As executive vice-president of a large bank in a metropolitan area, he carries heavy responsibilities, but he takes time for his church; he practices tithing. Although my friend's father is well beyond retirement age and requires attention, this splendid churchman and his wife have also adopted two elderly women in a nearby retirement home and joyously attend to their needs.

This contagious Christian handed me a lovely piece of white wood about the size of a half dollar which he frequently gives to confused individuals. On the front is printed in red letters TUIT; on the back is this statement: "I will put God first in my life when I get a-round tuit."

Following breakfast in his home, he turned to Scripture —*The New English Bible*—and read two passages. The first was Psalm 117. The second reading was from Revelation 3:14 ff., a description of the church at Laodicea. The key sentence in that paragraph of lament is, "I know all your ways; you are neither hot nor cold. How I wish you were either hot or cold!" My host remarked, "These are good starters for the day."

To be alive is to be in pilgrimage. Life is movement from where we are to where God would have us minister. This kind of commitment is adventuresome; it is not always structurally sound or financially defensible, but it is exceedingly rewarding.

The story of Jesus is the story of ascension. He was forever moving forward and upward through difficulty and discouragement. His pilgrimage was necessary and suggests what is required of every disciple. To be alive is to attain a higher altitude of spirit, to experience advancement, to share vision, and to nurture hope.

One of the distressing realities of our day is that society seems to reward those who follow protocol rather than pioneers with eyes fixed on beckoning horizons.

Like any journey, life is dangerous, filled with difficulties and excessive costs. Credit cards are not acceptable! The essence of one's character and courage is reflected in the tempo he maintains, the tilt of his heart, and the enjoyment of the journey.

To be alive is to be committed to Christ, his teachings, and his example. If one has been committed to an institution, we know what it means. If one declines our invitation for lunch on grounds that he has another commitment, we comprehend. When analysts refer to the nation's military and financial commitments in various areas of the world, we hope we understand.

Christian commitment is similar; we place our lives in the lap of the Lord, not in idleness, fear, or isolation, but in recognition of his will, love, and trust. Commitment is responding to Christ's call and accepting the abundant life. It is betting one's life there is a tomorrow!

While chairing a committee on the Christian ministry, conducting interviews prior to ordination, I was greatly impressed by one young man, thirty years of age, who had formerly taught school. While worshiping at church one Sunday, he was moved by the Spirit to prepare for the pastoral ministry. Married, with two children to support, on an income of three thousand dollars a year, he returned to seminary. When I asked him why he wanted to preach, he replied with humility but certainty, "I have found the abundant life and want to share it."

To be alive is to surrender to a higher will. Contrary to physical and mental combat, spiritual surrender involves confession of failure and assumes the sensitive posture of openness.

In his book, *A New Song*, Pat Boone relives events associated with his austere upbringing in Donelson, Tennessee —high school, shoplifting, early marriage, and his rise to fame. Even so, this direct descendant of Daniel Boone was restless, struggling to discover vocation and mission. All the while he preached in the Church of Christ and taught in their Sunday school.

His phenomenal rise to stardom bristled with problems. Eventually his marriage was in jeopardy; at one time Pat Boone owed two million dollars. With great humility he shares experiences from lean spiritual years.

Evaluating his difficulties, his inability to make and maintain a satisfactory contact with God, Pat concluded, "I wanted a confirmation before I'd made a commitment." This is a universal confession, the story of your life and mine. We want benefits without labor, freedom without discipline, happiness without disappointment, peace without conflict, and spiritual victories without surrender.

Once Pat Boone yielded to Christ, his career escalated; he began to sing "A New Song!" Like David, he could exclaim, "O sing to the Lord a new song, for he has done marvelous things" (Ps. 98:1, RSV).

To be alive is to be driven and sustained by certainty. There is a confidence, not arrogance, that characterizes those who answer Jesus' call, "Follow me."

In *Something Beautiful for God*, Malcolm Muggeridge refers to Mother Teresa of Calcutta as "blest with certainties." This saintly soul, struggling against inconceivable odds, is committed to bringing light, hope, and love to derelicts of India. A growing confidence in God and faith in the presence of Christ keep her going. She claims that whenever a homeless child cries she hears the Babe in Bethlehem.

Certainty is one of the obviously missing ingredients in modern culture. Traditions are laughed at; morals and ethics which once seemed so correct are fragmented if not ignored. Everything is up for grabs. Christian certainty suggests that one's faith in Christ must be visible, active, and contagious. While faith may be a gift, it usually emanates from love and discipline. Life is not only a matter of birth and preparation, it is a discipline that keeps one in tune with God, history, the contemporary scene, family, community, and the Christian faith.

Demographers are constantly reminding us that population is outstripping food and production. It is estimated that the human population of the globe in 6000 B.C. was about five million and perhaps required a million years to grow from two and one-half million to five million. The population of the world did not reach five hundred million until eight thousand years later—1650. It reached one billion one hundred years later. Then the population was doubled every two hundred years. Now the population is doubling every thirty-seven years.

If the present birth rate continues, nine hundred years from now the population will be sixty million billion people. This is one hundred persons for each square yard of the earth's surface. Conjure, if you can, the problems of God's children living in inconceivable situations—crowded, ill-fed, ill-housed, seldom loved. If we would live spaciously and sensitively, we must see our world in perspective. R. F. Francoeur helps us to comprehend more realistically the inequities plaguing mankind by reducing proportionately the three billion inhabitants of the earth to a community of one hundred souls.

In this simulated world there would be six American citizens; ninety-four would be natives of other countries. The six Americans, however, would own half of all the money. The fortunate six American citizens would have access to 72 percent of the food. Life expectancy of the Americans would be seventy years; the other ninety-four people could expect to live only thirty-nine years.

In this geometrical community there would be nine Protestants and twenty-five Catholics. Only thirty-three would come from countries where Christianity is taught. Less than half would have heard the name of Christ, but the majority of the ninety-four would know of Lenin. In their shops would be at least two Communist documents which outsell the Bible. From this compact community comes word that by the year 2000 one out of every two persons will be Chinese.

How is one to live in a world so divided geographically, politically, economically, religiously, and ideologically? Who will battle for brotherhood, equity, and justice? Who will demonstrate love?

Life is not so much a matter of mathematical exactness as it is mental and spiritual inclusiveness; it is not doing a sum, it is painting a picture.

Being made in the image of God, man is a synthesis of all that we know and imagine. Dr. Helmut Thielicke, German theologian and preacher, declares the parable of the prodigal son affords valuable insight into the meaning of life. This condemning and challenging story has a message far beyond the usual moral lessons.

This well-born, well-reared young man decided he wanted to experience life for himself. He asked for his inheritance, and to his surprise, he received it. Then he took up residence in a different community.

Why did he wish to leave home? Could it be he was smothered by comfort and affection? Was he so much a part of a well-regulated family that he never became a person?

Let us assume the young man did not leave home to sow wild oats but to find himself. He wanted freedom! However, he soon discovered that freedom is a paradox, that one is most free when he learns he is not free, but responsible for himself, others, and to God. Money and friends gone, the wanderer found himself in misery and solitude.

As Thielicke asserts, the young man, who went out looking for himself, actually lost himself! He was overwhelmed, and while in this pensive mood, he thought of his well-disciplined home and, strangely enough, yearned for it. He tightened his belt and started trudging homeward. The prodigal did not experience the meaning of life until he encountered his father and asked forgiveness.

The waiting father embraced and welcomed home his son. Reconciliation achieved, there was a feast of love. "Bring quickly the best robe, and put it on him; and put a ring on his hand, and shoes on his feet; and bring the fatted calf and kill it, and let us eat and make merry; for this my son was dead, and is alive again; he was lost, and is found" (Luke 15:22–24, RSV).

The gospel is a picture of life, a portrait of Jesus Christ. The gospel is an invitation to live. "I came that they may have life, and have it abundantly" (John 10:10, RSV). "He who has the Son has life; he who has not the Son of God has not life" (1 John 5:12, RSV). Living is too brief, too serious, to take lightly these proclamations. They require immediate, consistent, and enthusiastic response. To live is more than escaping death, celebrating birthdays, rearing a family, achieving retirement. To live is to find purpose. There is power in Christian purpose.

To live is to find ways of sharing the Good News of God's love. Jesus warned that the good life cannot be protected or squandered in selfishness; it cannot be stored in lockboxes at the bank. Life, he taught, can be saved only through service—use!

Being in New Haven, Connecticut, the fall of 1971, I dropped by to see my admired teacher, Dr. Luther A. Weigle, dean and Sterling professor emeritus of Yale University Divinity School.

As I approached his home, my mind replayed his many involvements and contributions. His distinguished leadership in the church and academic communities, training of teachers and preachers, productive writer, Bible translator, his role in the formation of the National Council of Churches—all loomed before me. My most treasured memory, however, was my recollection of Dean Weigle as friend and available counselor.

He was watching the World Series on television when I arrived. I chided him for substituting sport for scholarship! Our reminiscings included the oft-told story that followed a demanding day. The dean had bowed his head to offer grace at the family evening meal and politely said, "Weigle speaking."

I asked his evaluation of the New English and Jerusalem Bibles. With ease and enthusiasm he cited differences in texts, quoting briefly from original sources to substantiate

31

his preference for the Revised Standard Version of Scripture.

Referring to a spate of contemporary problems, he remarked, "I am glad I have lived my life . . ." This was not a gesture of weak resignation, cynicism, or despair, but rather the dilemma of a man whose mind was sharp but whose physical strength was waning. His demeanor and voice registered regret that he was unable to participate more vigorously in the struggle for the minds of men.

Here was a giant, ninety-two years of age, with an assortment of ailments, yet as current as the score of the World Series, proud and grateful for life as an ancient prophet. To visit with such a contagious Christian as Luther A. Weigle was to recapture the greatness of life. His grace and good cheer confirmed his faith in the journey.

After thirty-six years and the appearance of 1,864 issues, *Life* magazine concluded operations December 29, 1972. As would be expected under the circumstances, it was a swan-song format. However, that which caught my eye was the promotional card—so prominent in periodicals these days—attached between pages 72 and 73, reading, "Please start sending me *Life*."

This is more than a technical inaccuracy, too costly to eliminate. It is in reality every man's prayer: "Dear God, please keep sending me life."

2

The Trauma of Waiting

Our patience will achieve more than our force.

Edmund Burke

Learn to labor and to wait.
Henry Wadsworth Longfellow

Wait for the Lord; be strong, and let your heart take courage; yea, wait for the Lord!

Psalm 27:14, RSV

So that you may not be sluggish, but imitators of those who through faith and patience inherit the promises.

Hebrews 6:12, RSV

We are in a hurry; God is not. There were fourteen generations between Abraham and David, fourteen more between David and deportation to Babylon; and still another fourteen generations before the appearance of the Messiah. God could wait!

Because of Jewish orientation and his sense of history, Matthew took pains to trace the lineage of Jesus. Preparation for Jesus' coming required centuries. Ancient believers waited in hope, not idleness, in expectation, not anxiety.

Americans are impetuous and seldom take time to be friendly, enjoy nature, contemplate options. We live in a bustle. The popular aphorist, Eric Hoffer, claims the temper of our time is impatience. "Tomorrow has become a dirty word. The future is now, and hope has turned into desire."

An automated society has little appreciation of patience. It is geared to productivity, not to people. Everyone is playing leapfrog, concentrating on the ultimate objective, leaving little time for meditation, visitation, or growth.

Many leaders of emerging countries expect rights, resources, and recognition that once were reserved for patient pathfinders. They, like minority groups in America, are tired of waiting; they want action.

It is hard for Americans to wait. We are calibrated with the computer, cloverleaf, and airplane. Accustomed to instantaneous responses and messages, we move at an accelerated pace, expecting the same from others—including God!

Beyond automation, personal ambition, and schedule, we inevitably encounter experiences we can neither manipulate nor expedite. Life has ways of bringing to a screaming stop the most energetic, independent of individuals. However resentful of the interruption, however costly the cause, there are moments when one can only wait.

Sadly I recall my involvement in a hazing incident in college. It occurred after the last football game of the season. Following a weird and frightening tradition—involving physical torture—freshmen were accorded recognition due college men. Sensing alienation among a few freshmen, a number of us went to investigate. The encounter was rough, violent. One boy lost his eye.

Despite the hour of the night, we called the campus physician who took the injured student to the hospital where surgery was performed. When apprised of the extent of injury, the lad asked if I would stay by him through the operation. I nodded in the affirmative. Quickly he added, "I mean in the operating room, too." Again I gave him my word.

Although in an unsophisticated hospital years ago, my desire to honor the patient's request posed problems. Agreements were reached. Gowned, nervous, and perspiring, I was relegated to a harmless spot. The sight, sounds, and smell of the operating room were nauseating. Later, when I was permitted to visit my friend, his first question was, "Did you stay with me?" I was proud to report I had. What if I had not waited?

Judge Roy D. Williams, Booneville, Missouri, received his diploma from Kemper Military School at age ninety. In 1899 he participated in a protest march. Tents were pitched in the city park. The students won! An unpopular order was rescinded. However, at commencement several young men were denied their diplomas, including Roy Williams.

On the one hundred twenty-seventh anniversary of the founding of Kemper Military School, May 1971, in special ceremonies the judge received his diploma. He had not waited for wrongs to be righted. He neither pitied himself nor pouted over the situation but continued his pursuit of law and his service to Missouri.

Waiting is always difficult. One cannot hurry the dawn by watching the clock, speed up the message by sitting near the telephone, or deliver a baby by pacing the floor. Waiting is an intricate and inevitable part of life, a test of patience and character.

Waiting has its own peculiar dimensions of time. When running late, off schedule, waiting at the traffic light seems interminable, as does the expected telephone call or letter or the emergence of the surgeon from the operating room.

Delays are irksome. Eyes of the world were fixed on Cape Kennedy. The final moon shot in the Apollo program was scheduled to lift off at 7:53 P.M. EST, December 6, 1972. Public media had alerted readers and viewers to the night spectacular. Prelaunch reports indicated the smoothest of all countdowns was in progress, including those in the Mercury and Gemini series.

After arduous preparations for the mission, Astronauts Navy Captain Eugene A. Cernan, Dr. Harrison H. Schmitt, geologist, and Navy Commander Ronald E. Evans went through the final ritual of boarding the huge space vehicle. All signals were "go." Then dramatically at T minus thirty seconds, an automatic detector shut off the count. It was the first hold due to technical difficulties in the Apollo program.

Concern for the astronauts heightened as one contemplated their predicament, perched atop the thirty-six-story rocket with more than one million gallons of supercold liquid oxygen, liquid hydrogen, and kerosene aboard. The four-hundred-fifty-million-dollar trip of approximately 488,760 miles, twelve days, sixteen hours, thirty-one minutes was delayed. These phenomenal men were psyched up, ready to go, but they had to wait. Dr. Schmitt had waited seven years for a moon mission assignment, and with thirty seconds left in countdown, the word was *hold*. Hold they did for two hours and forty minutes. Waiting before the world!

Waiting is an unscheduled part of our lives. We wait for the dentist and the doctor; we wait for promotions; we queue up to check out at the grocery counter, to board the plane, and practically everywhere except church. We wait for the holiday, anniversary, anticipated event. Nervously we wait for the children to return home with the automobile, for the result of laboratory tests, and for the appreciation of a security.

No phase of the long Vietnam trucidation was more vexing than the ambivalence surrounding status of captured servicemen. Relatives of missing prisoners of war knew the pathos of waiting, working, sleeping alone. Wives of many unfortunate military men in Southeast Asia lived in limbo, not knowing if they were widowed or married. Some POW's returned to find they had been divorced.

In its December 7, 1970 issue, *Life* shared a number of interviews with POW wives. Referring to her children, one said, "It must be hard for my husband because he doesn't have them to touch, like I have."

Another lamenting, irritated wife exclaimed, "Why me? Why the hell me?"

Still another reported on her frustrated daughter who cried two and one-half years for her father. The equally crushed mother finally snapped, "Kid, shut up. He isn't here. What do you want from me?"

An unusually philosophical wife of a prisoner commented, "Well, I can look back and say 'All right, my husband has been gone five years, but have they been total wastes?' No. Finally I was able to get my master's, which I couldn't do because we were always moving. Finally we have been able to save some money. Finally we have been able to get a home. You have to look for the salvation in this."

After ten years of fighting, death of two and one-quarter million people, two thousand missing Americans, astronomical costs, accords were signed in twenty-nine minutes. Then began more agonizing days of waiting, wondering, hoping the name of a loved one would be released and the date of arrival home announced.

Waiting is costly. Sometimes we wait too long to do what we ought to do. The parable of the rich fool brings priorities and values assessments into sharp focus. " 'Fool! This night your soul is required of you' " (Luke 12:20, RSV).

Farming is an old and honored vocation, doubtless the oldest. Many who have no use for professions, appreciate the farmer. The rich fool described by Jesus had apparently come honestly by his fortune. There is no indication he exploited his neighbor, no evidence he squeezed small competitors out of business. He was clever in the care of soil and in the production of crops.

His yield exceeded all expectations. The farmer viewed options. " 'What shall I do . . . ? . . . I will do this: I will pull down my barns, and build larger ones; and there I will store all my grain and my goods. And I will say to my soul, Soul, you have ample goods laid up for many years; take your ease, eat, drink, be merry' " (Luke 12:17–19, RSV).

Although the successful operator solved the harvest problem, he failed to gain a new perspective; he failed to reckon with God. His syllogism included "my barns," "my grain," "my goods," "myself" for many years. Not once did he voice gratitude for his success.

God became annoyed. " 'Fool! This night your soul is required of you; and the things you have prepared, whose will they be?' " (Luke 12:20, RSV). The prestigious farmer was a fool because he waited too long to acknowledge and worship God!

Nations, institutions, and communities frequently wait too long to respond to rumor, suspicion, fact, conditions. To be sure, there is always the danger of overreaction, but an equally perilous sin is waiting too long to listen, to act.

Visitors to Honolulu usually see Pearl Harbor. Two hundred years ago Hawaiians called it *Wae Momi*, "Water of Pearl." In 1861 the United States Navy constructed a fueling station in Honolulu. By 1916 it was the tenth most important naval base in the world. Eventually it became the Fourteenth Naval District, center of Pacific operations. However, we chiefly remember Pearl Harbor as scene of the surprise, dastardly air attack by the Japanese on Sunday morning, December 7, 1941, at six o'clock. On that infamous day, 2,335 American servicemen lost their lives; 1,143 were wounded.

Eighteen of the ninety-seven ships along "Battleship Row" were sunk. The *Arizona* sank in nine minutes with eleven hundred men aboard. To this day this rusting hulk —now a memorial—continues to give off oil, even as memory of the attack alienates thoughtful citizens.

Years before the assault, Japan's military experts wrote,

"In case we are forced to go to war with America, we will attack at Pearl Harbor on Sunday." Why? Japan knew the habits of Americans over weekends, especially military personnel away from home. When our Signal Corps flashed warnings on that memorable day, they were ignored until it was too late.

Whatever the crisis, it has to be severe for Americans to respond. Will we wait too long to avert another global conflict? Will we wait too long to establish and practice more equitable standards of living? Will we wait too long to heed signals of death from our environment? How long will we wait before making the church the Christian community it was commissioned to be?

Is it not true that many of us wait too long to strengthen family relationships? We wait too long to be good mates, good parents, good members of a united family until there is a tragedy.

A twentieth-century version of the parable of the rich fool emanates from Montreal. Two sisters inherited a sizeable fortune, and the younger one expressed a desire to travel. Her wishes were quickly squelched by the older sister, "We don't have that much money." They bought a store on the Gaspé Peninsula.

One day two men from Florida stopped to make purchases. Their presence stimulated the younger woman's desire to travel. Again she suggested, "Let's close down for a month or so . . . go to Miami. It might be fun to use some of the lipstick we sell . . ."

"No," was the reply. "People would start trading elsewhere and we would lose our business."

A decade passed. Business continued profitably. Eventually the restless sister asked, "What is the point of making more money? Let's sell out and take a trip to California, perhaps Mexico. We might even meet a couple of fellows and get married."

"No one would pay what the store is worth," replied the pessimistic partner. However, the following year they received an offer on the property, but turned it down.

After closing the store one cold January night, the unhappy sister, still in her fifties, walked home. She fell on the ice and never recovered.

The older woman closed the store. She buried her sister in an elaborate bronze casket. In due time, and with legal manipulation, the guilt-ridden one gained permission to disinter the body and move it to California. The living sister flew to the West Coast in a private plane with a beautiful casket as companion. Eventually, through the assistance of an influential attorney, she procured another disinterment permit and flew with the casket to Mexico City.

We all have our little caskets—choices, regrets, promises never fulfilled, vows broken, lives destroyed.

Richard Speck murdered eight nurses in Chicago, July 14, 1966. The brutality outraged America. On June 5, 1967, Speck was sentenced to die in the electric chair for his crimes. Boldly he declared, "People deserve the chair when they kill somebody."

After years of legal maneuvering and waiting, finally in November of 1972 Judge Richard F. Fitzgerald of Cook County (Chicago) Circuit Court, presiding in a Peoria, Illinois, courtroom said, "The only fair and just sentence in this case is one in which the defendant would be confined for life." Whereupon the judge sentenced Speck to 400–1200 years in prison, eight consecutive terms of 50–150 years—one sentence for each death. Although there is no possible way the culprit can hope to fulfill the longevity of the punishment, knowledge of his debt to unborn centuries reverberating in his mind, together with memories of the eight murdered girls, must be an unbearable weight with which to wait for eternity.

Whatever the situation—postponement, interruption—it is not to be compared with waiting for a loved one to die. Helpless waiting is enervating and unnerving. The Reverend John R. Claypool, pastor, Broadway Baptist Church, Fort Worth, Texas, shares the tedium and exhausting experience of waiting with his daughter, Laura Lue, victim of leukemia.

The days were long; the nights, lonely. The pastor-father found it difficult—as many of us have—to practice what he preached, to live his sermons. Courageously he demonstrated it can be done. Beautifully he shared his experiences with his congregation. Mr. Claypool found great comfort and strength from Scripture and prayer, especially Isaiah's great words, "They who wait for the Lord shall renew their strength, they shall mount up with wings like eagles, they shall run and not be weary, they shall walk and not faint" (40:31, RSV). To be sure, the sorrowing father did not sprout wings nor was he ready for a foot race, but he was given strength to endure, to offer a sip of water, to utter words of encouragement and love.

A friend was smitten by a massive stroke. All day the family waited in the hospital. Upon hearing the news, I joined them in the physicians' lounge where I offered prayer. Later on the elevator a surgeon who was in the wings and who heard the prayer introduced himself, saying, "Life and death are only eyelashes apart. We see it every day and all we can do is wait."

Waiting for death would render one inarticulate were it not for the knowledge of God's presence and his awareness of our deep need. How well I remember the homegoing of my mother. This saintly soul always expressed the wish to die at home, in her own bed, and she did. Unlike her sweet, gentle life, her death was a prolonged, painful ordeal. There was nothing we could do but be attentive, present, comforting. The time came when she did not recognize her family; yet her heart was strong. In those moments we prayed she would be spared further suffering.

Miss Anne Sedgwick, the novelist, was bedfast at age seventy. She endured excruciating pain and constant distress. If she sat up, her ribs collapsed making it difficult to breathe; if she lay down, she could not swallow the necessary fluids every thirty minutes. Even so, she said, "Life is a queer struggle, but life is beautiful to me. There is joy in knowing that I lie in the hands of God."

An inspiring and knowledgeable Christian of our generation was C. S. Lewis. Oxford trained and oriented, this master of oral communication, lecturer, author, radio broadcaster, was late embracing Christianity. Lewis was not married until in his fifties. Shortly afterward, Joy, his wife, developed cancer and died a slow, painful death.

After her homegoing he wrote *A Grief Observed*. At first he acknowledged his disappointment in what his religion had meant in the crisis. Later, with his usual perception, he diagnosed the problem as being personal, one of expectation more than experience. When what he wanted did not happen, he almost lost sight of what was happening.

God may not cure the loved one whose life is ebbing away, but he may cure our sense of anxiety and fear and enable us to face great loss with grace and faith. In this connection, Josef Pieper maintains there are two devastating forms of temptation: one, when we become frustrated with God, impatient, take things in our own hands, frequently exploding with anger and retaliation; second, to give up, sink deeper into despair. Waiting has a way of making us presumptuous or despondent.

In *Despair—a Moment or a Way of Life?* C. Stephen Evans maintains man has become a conglomeration of functions, small cogs in giant wheels of modern society. Caught up in the machinery of activities and responsibilities, man needs to be awakened to a realization of humanity. To understand hope, then, we must understand despair, differentiating between despair as a moment in life and as a way of life. The Danish philosopher, Sören Kierkegaard, said, "Despair is sickness unto death." Despair is more than mental depression; it grips the entire being.

An unfortunate soul heard Jesus was en route to Jairus' home to attend his ill daughter. Hoping to see him, she waited. According to Scripture she suffered from a hemorrhage. For twelve long years her illness not only made her miserable but separated her from society.

Consider what normally can be accomplished in twelve years! All this person had seen of any consequence was the wasting away of her body. At last she heard the commotion of a jubilant multitude approaching, the laughter of children running ahead, the sight of expectant people. As the central figure became more visible, she focused on him, believing in her heart if she touched him she would be whole.

"Who was it that touched me?" (Luke 8:45, RSV) Jesus asked. Peter and others told him that many had brushed against him in the crowd. This answer was unsatisfactory; the Lord felt power leaving him.

When the trembling woman realized she would be identified, she confessed. The Master declared, "Daughter, your faith has made you well; go in peace" (Luke 8:48, RSV). Waiting twelve years to be healed; waiting twelve years to touch Jesus!

Ministers recognize given types of people, whether in joy or sorrow. Some have a much greater tolerance for pain, and a greater capacity for understanding and patience than others. Some cannot endure prolonged physical or emotional strain. As the inevitable approaches, some withdraw, become uncommunicative, if not bitter. Some are rebellious and judgmental. Others are so stoic in their acceptance that there are no signs of hurt, no tears.

Individuals who find it difficult to communicate in moments of great loss and need, who feel that weeping is an indication of weakness, often collapse after hospitalization and memorial services and frequently become patients themselves. Not hysteria, but genuine weeping and the overflowing of sorrow are essential to total well-being; it is a necessary prelude to the recapturing of one's emotional equilibrium.

Jesus experienced every conceivable type of sorrow. He knew his ministry would jeopardize his life; yet he continued in patience and love, waiting for leadership of the Spirit, praying alone. He also wept in face of sorrow.

You will remember his encounter with friends in Bethany following Lazarus' death. Martha said, " 'Lord, if you had been here, my brother would not have died.' . . . Jesus said to her, 'Your brother will rise again' " (John 11:21,23, RSV). Martha replied she knew he would at the last day. Then Jesus uttered words of assurance, "I am the resurrection and the life; he who believes in me, though he die, yet shall he live, and whoever lives and believes in me shall never die. Do you believe this?" (John 11:25–26, RSV).

Observing the tears of Mary and Martha and seeing that many in the crowd were also weeping, "Jesus wept" (John 11:35, RSV). This prompted some of the Jews to say, "See how he loved him!" (John 11:36, RSV). Anyone who has misgivings about crying in such circumstances should re-read this story.

Following his resurrection, Jesus instructed his disciples, "Do not leave Jerusalem, but wait for the gift my Father promised, that I told you about" (Acts 1:4, TEV). While they were all together in one place, "Suddenly a sound came from heaven like the rush of a mighty wind, and it filled all the house where they were sitting" (Acts 2:2, RSV). Instantly, disillusioned disciples became men of power and courage. They received the spirit to become! Pentecost marked the end of waiting and the beginning of the visible church.

A precious secret of life is learning to live one day at a time. This can be extremely difficult. We have moments of depression, discouragement, frustration when life appears beamed against us; no amount of spiritual provision seems adequate. This may be God's moment; wait and pray. Be sensitive to change; be open, honest, and trustful.

Robert Louis Stevenson, whose patience and strength were frequently challenged, once remarked, "Every man can get through until nightfall." Tomorrow is another day. This is the essence of hope!

Sir William Ousler urged his students to "live in day-tight compartments." The famous British physician maintained that burdens of yesterday added to the fears of tomorrow carried today will break the strongest. Learning to endure trials, anxieties, and waiting is essential to contagious Christian living. Not even Jesus' disciples understood; they went to sleep while he struggled to keep alive his faith.

As a distance runner, our coach did many things to impress us with the importance of recognizing one's pace. Sometimes we would run with a stop watch; sometimes we would be asked to guess the pace of a teammate. Without a watch or a teammate the coach would call out time for each lap. After months of training and experience, it is amazing how one learns his pace. Good runners do not worry about the last lap; they concentrate on the challenge of the moment.

Life is like a foot race. It requires stamina and a sense of timing. The rhythm of joy and sorrow, thrust and retardation, working and waiting, eating and sleeping must be carefully calibrated or we lose the delicate balance so necessary in developing patience, courage, and strength.

We salute those who continue their work while waiting health developments; the courage of those who live with private agony inspires us. Stewart Alsop, popular columnist, gave an intimate account of his bout with leukemia in *Newsweek*, July 31, 1972. With remarkable candor he shared what it is like to live with a "life-threatening disease."

"I wish I could claim that the past year has given me profound spiritual insights but it hasn't." Mr. Alsop said that above all, the experience taught him how nice people are. Most individuals live behind "a thick outer tegument, or carapace" which separates. "The threat of death breaks the carapace." During the early days of his illness, Alsop ran across this sentence from Winston Churchill: "For the rest, live dangerously; take life as it comes; dread naught; all will be well."

Centuries before this scintillating sentence, the psalmist declared: "Wait for the Lord; be strong, and let your heart take courage; yea, wait for the Lord!" (Ps. 27:14, RSV). The author knew struggle and stress; he also knew the meaning of confidence and trust. His faith was unshakable.

Jesus substantiated and magnified the psalmist many times: "My Father, if it be possible, let this cup pass from me; nevertheless, not as I will, but as thou wilt" (Matt. 26:39, RSV). The Lord waited and prayed, but the cup did not pass.

Later with enviable confidence Jesus said, "Father, into thy hands I commit my spirit!" (Luke 23:46, RSV). This is the epitome of trust.

The Christian waits, not in relaxed resignation or in tranquilized anxiety, but in disciplined meditation for the stirring of the Spirit. He prays for God's will to be known, for perception to see it, and for the grace to accept it.

Visualize old Simeon, frail in body, hopeful in heart, carrying the burdens of age gallantly. He silhouetted

Israel's past—its faith and righteousness, piety and hope. Anointed by the expectation of the Messiah, the saintly soul greeted each day with joyous anticipation. Unknown to Simeon, Jesus had been born a scant seven miles to the south of the Holy City, Bethlehem. Joseph and Mary brought the child to Jerusalem and presented him in the temple. Nudged by the Spirit, Simeon entered at the same hour.

When the old man saw the beautiful child, he remembered how God enters the world and human hearts in unsuspecting ways. Recognizing the babe as the promised one, he took him in his arms and prayed, "Lord, now lettest thou thy servant depart in peace, according to thy word; for mine eyes have seen thy salvation which thou hast prepared in the presence of all peoples, a light for revelation to the Gentiles, and for glory to thy people Israel" (Luke 2:29–32, RSV). Simeon was compensated for believing and waiting. He saw the Lord!

Whether waiting with parents of a two-year-old to die with Race syndrome, a mother to go with cancer, or a grandfather suffocating from emphysema, life—like a well-written book—is variously punctuated. While there are recurring question marks in the daily manuscript, the infinite hand of wisdom and mercy continues to write— *love!*

Writing from acquaintance with controversy, bereavement, and blindness, the great seventeenth-century English poet, John Milton, said, "They also serve who only stand and wait."

3

Living with Loneliness

Solitude verifies; isolation kills.
Joseph Roux

We wait in the quietness for some
centering moment that will redefine,
reshape, and refocus our lives.
Howard Thurman

I am not alone, for the Father is with me.
Jesus, John 16:32, RSV

To whom can any man say—Here I am!
Behold me in my nakedness, my wounds,
     my secret grief,
My despair, my betrayal, my pain,
My tongue which cannot express any
     sorrow,
My terror, my abandonment.

Listen to me for a day—an hour! A
     moment!
Lest I expire in my terrible wilderness,
     my lonely silence!

O God, is there no one to listen . . . ? [1]
Taylor Caldwell

These beautiful words are perennially haunting and time-less in relevance, compassion, condemnation. They indicate the most serious of all credibility gaps—anonymity.

Ann Landers' syndicated column is carried in some 688 newspapers throughout the world. She has a reading audience of fifty-four million people. Her mail comes from truck drivers, factory workers, waiters, parents, college professors, executives, physicians, attorneys, clergymen.

"The fact that the column has been a success," she says, "underscores, for me at least, the central tragedy of our society . . . the loneliness . . . the fear that bedevils, cripples, and paralyzes so many of us."

It is ironically disturbing that in a world whose population doubles every thirty-seven years, individuals should be lonely. This reality was substantiated for me a few years ago when I disembarked at Roberts Field, Liberia. Walking toward the airport, suddenly I was aware of being alone in Africa! Mine was the only white face in the crowd. How comforting to hear my name spoken by a tall, hand-some African who politely handed me an envelope bearing an invitation to lunch with a black Baptist minister in Mon-rovia.

Loneliness is a universal experience. It knows no culture, geography, race, sex, or age. Everyone is lonely at one time or another. Some, by their attitudes, acts, or posture, separate themselves from their peers. Others become lonely because they have been neglected, forgotten, or victimized.

---

1. Used by permission of author.

Living with Loneliness

In reading the giants of history, one glimpses profiles of loneliness—Moses, Elijah, Jeremiah, Hosea, Paul, St. Francis of Assisi, Martin Luther, John Wesley, Albert Schweitzer, and Jesus of Nazareth. The pursuit of excellence separates individuals. Dedication to mission invites loneliness.

At times Jesus was a lonely man. Consider the cross! How ignored he must have felt. The cheering crowds of Palm Sunday—like most human relations—had deteriorated into a howling, angry mob, intent on inconceivable punishment. In a dreadful moment the Master cried: "My God, my God, why hast thou forsaken me?" (Matt. 27:46, RSV). Not even our Lord was spared the anguish of loneliness and pain.

Throughout the world, men stand shoulder to shoulder, work under the same roof, wait for transportation, queue up for service but do not know one another. There are people everywhere; yet there is so little empathy and love.

There is a fascinating sentence in Scripture: "I am like a vulture of the wilderness, like an owl of the waste places; I lie awake, I am like a lonely bird on the house-top" (Ps. 102:6–7, RSV). In varying degrees we all share despair, frustration, and loneliness.

A young man stood on the ledge of a seventeen-story building above Fifth Avenue in New York City, obviously desperate. Police and firemen sought to rescue him, but at last he exclaimed, "I am a lonely man. I wish someone could convince me life is worth living." Then he jumped.

The family is also involved. Caught in unpredictable change, it is running out of time. The family is no longer the center of economic, social, and religious supportive-ness. Too often it is a harassed household of strangers, desperately trying to maintain different schedules and life-styles.

Mothers of children from six to seventeen years of age, employed outside the home, aggregate 48 percent of the total adult female population in America. Irrespective of why mothers work, thousands of children come home daily to maids, babysitters, notes, or quiet houses. Children growing up without parents is unnatural and may prove to be a costly experiment. Moreover, fathers work long days; many travel, home for the weekend and gone again.

Active parents can be lonely people. Frequently their duties are so heavy and varied that they are separated in their coverage of responsibilities—mother attending one meeting, father another.

My wife and I popped in one evening on a couple who had visited our church. Knowing they had small children, we waited later than usual to call. Even so, they were in the midst of getting their littles ones settled when we arrived.

They greeted us warmly, expressing the hope we would stay and visit. We broke all rules—stayed three hours! They were lonely and hungry for Christian fellowship. Their questions concerning the church were provocative, stimulating, reassuring.

Moonlighting is common. At least 3.6 million workers in the United States have more than one job. Add to the diversity and involvement of parents, erosion of values, exaggerated significance of gadgets, materialistic motivations, and one begins to visualize great chasms in community.

Teen-agers have their hectic schedules and frequently

find themselves alone amid pressing activities and difficult decisions. How can continuity between generations be maintained without the presence of one another, harmony and warmth, trust and teachings of the home?

Little wonder there are said to be 6.5 million emotionally disturbed children in America. Sitting on the board of an institution dedicated to their care, I was astonished to perceive their loneliness and their inability to articulate need.

As if these cataclysmic facts were not sufficiently alarming, 1974 statistics indicate there are 5,963,000 divorced persons in the United States, 1,855,000 widowers, and 9,814,000 widows. These figures silhouette considerable sorrow, fear, and loneliness!

We are also witnessing a retirement revolution. If demographic reports are correct, there are more than twenty-two million Americans sixty-five years of age and older, many of whom live away from their families. At least five million elderly Americans live alone. The number increases by one thousand a day. Nursing homes are crowded with pitiful, lonely souls.

Add to this pyramid of loneliness about twenty million refugees scattered throughout the world who, for the most part, are victims of power politics, other men's decisions and mistakes. Twenty million approximates the population of New York City, St. Louis, Houston, and Detroit! Moreover, there are one million refugees living in our country, half of whom are from Cuba, others from Hong Kong, Indonesia, Vietnam, and Czechoslovakia. This is a dimension of loneliness few Americans can comprehend.

Loneliness wears many faces and calls at unexpected

hours. The psalmist knew this: "Turn thou to me, and be gracious to me; for I am lonely and afflicted" (Ps. 25:16, RSV). Who isn't?

Loneliness is discovering you are an illegitimate child.

Loneliness is the first day of kindergarten; a boy's initial stay away from home; a freshman in college; a country girl searching for a job in the city, working in strange surroundings where procedures, people, and temptations are different.

Loneliness is dropping the winning touchdown pass in the end zone; flying deep to an outfielder to end the World Series.

Loneliness is learning that parents are divorcing and you will be awarded by the court to one, with only occasional visits with the other.

Loneliness is a mother away from her children; a father in a motel on a business trip.

Loneliness is a conscientious objector caught up in the euphoria and ambiguities of war, shunned and talked about because of his convictions.

Loneliness is being black in a white man's society; poor in a rich man's America; a minor in an adult world.

Loneliness is voting your conscience, knowing all the while your candidate does not have a chance to win.

Loneliness is living alone in a big house, enveloped by memories, surrounded by antiques.

Loneliness is waiting for surgery in the hospital knowing when you wake up—if you do—there will be no flowers in the room, no relative or friend to say, "I love you."

Loneliness is seeing your children grow up, marry, and move away; pictures and artifacts are still in their rooms and in more sensitive moments their voices are all but audible, but there are no faces, no hands to touch.

Loneliness is watching affluent Americans on television at a bar, then returning to one's dirty, rat-infested room in a ghetto.

Loneliness is hitchhiking five hundred miles with fifty cents in your pocket.

Loneliness is standing up to preach and people are not there; calling a church board meeting and there is no quorum.

Loneliness is setting foot on foreign soil without portfolio or letters of introduction.

Loneliness is waiting for a loved one to return from a business trip, job interview, the armed services, or school.

Loneliness is growing old in a society that ignores its aging.

Loneliness is declaring yourself psychologically destitute, forfeiting possessions, in order to qualify for and be marooned in the sickening aroma of a decaying garden, a geriatric home.

Loneliness is placing a telephone call and there is no answer; waiting for the postman and there is no mail.

Loneliness is praying and receiving no immediate answer.

Loneliness is watching your shadow bob along a busy street in a strange city where no one nods and no one speaks.

Loneliness—from the cradle to the grave—is life. It is a subtle and dangerous social disease. How shall we deal with it?

There is a striking difference between loneliness and aloneness. Loneliness is a ravenous enemy which eats away at integrity and happiness, weakens faith, and destroys creativity. This quiet intruder rearranges agenda, dilutes purpose, and fragments loyalties. Aloneness is a friend, a deliberate period of separation, the atmosphere of productivity, fountain of genuineness, altar of inspiration.

Early in 1971 a lonely forty-two-year-old widow, dying of cancer in Chattanooga, Tennessee, wrote a note to the paper. Among other things, she said, "I am so lonely— the nights are so long." Within four days she received 613 letters from fifty-two communities and six states. The result was miraculous. Her response? "I found there are people who are even lonelier than I am. I am now so busy answering my mail I haven't time to think about pain or loneliness."

Society is crowded with people who need to make this discovery. There is the shy girl hiding her self-consciousness, social ineptness, behind the mask of casualness punctuated by excessive drinking and smoking. A quiet man, in lieu of friends and proper motivation, withdraws to his room after work or walks the lonely streets at night. An aging person who, having lost zest for life, pulls down the shades and lives a detached, alienated existence.

Jesus knew what it was to be alone; in fact, he sought solitude where he could pray for guidance before making momentous decisions. He was alone in the wilderness save for the devil, alone in the Garden of Gethsemane while his insensitive disciples slept. He was alone on the cross except for God!

Periods of loneliness may be turned into moments of aloneness, inspiration, and challenge if we permit God to teach us about ourselves. As Edwin Markham, the American poet, declared, one can live a lifetime without knowing himself. To avoid reality, most of us watch everything and everybody; we become preoccupied and obsessed with things and cleverly shun ourselves. We need to rediscover identity. Confidence comes with the assurance that we are children of God; we are each different, of course, but precious, so valuable that God permitted his Son to die for us. We are heirs, not only of the earth, but also of eternity! Solitude, then, correctly interpreted and used, communicates personal worth and affords opportunity for growth and dedication.

"God is our refuge and strength, a very present help in trouble" (Ps. 46:1, RSV).

"Be still, and know that I am God. I am exalted among the nations, I am exalted in the earth!" (Ps. 46:10, RSV).

"In the world you have tribulation; but be of good cheer, I have overcome the world" (John 16:33, RSV).

"Lo, I am with you always, to the close of the age" (Matt. 28:20, RSV).

One may be lonely, but he need not be alone!

Solitude can be the wrestler's mat where one gains perspective, purpose, power.

Solitude can be the high court wherein one stands alone with himself, his Lord, probing, promising, rediscovering, recommitting self to the highest and best.

Solitude can be the impregnable chamber where one sorts and rearranges values and accepts life's beckoning horizons.

Solitude can be the teamster's whip that lashes out against

self-pity and complacency and stings one's conscience, summons energy that one may move forward with grace and wisdom to concentrate on worthwhile ventures.

There is a sense in which everything stands alone—the mysterious raindrop, the majestic isolation of one star from another, each tree growing according to design and destiny. Animals and birds live, fight, and die for themselves, even as do human beings. Separateness finds its ultimate culmination in man who is not only alone but knows it! Unlike other creatures, man inquires about his aloneness. Since he cannot escape it, how can he endure it?

God is aware of man's plight. In the story of creation we read: "Then the Lord God said, 'It is not good that the man should be alone; I will make him a helper fit for him' " (Gen. 2:18, RSV). The bodily separation of Adam and Eve not only confirmed their individuality, aloneness, though longing for each other, but God's recognition of each one's responsibility and guilt. The Lord listened separately to their excuses and pronounced separate afflictions.

Not even God can completely liberate man from his aloneness. Having made him ruler of the visible universe, he is, therefore, able to see it and through discipline, duty, and love, transcend it. In *The Eternal Now* Paul Tillich says the word *loneliness* is used to express the pain of being alone; *solitude* expresses the glory of being alone.

Loneliness following the separation or loss of one who enabled us to forget our aloneness is difficult to endure.

Those who have companions, status, sex, identity in the crowd—do they not also know the pangs of loneliness? There are those who choose the closets of isolation because they have accentuated their separateness by indulgence and exploitation; guilt becomes not only a barrier but a burden.

Some know the loneliness of love rejected. The awareness of inadequacies, being dropped or forgotten in favor of another, requires remarkable resiliency or one shuts himself off from the world. "Loneliness," said Tillich, "can be conquered only by those who can bear solitude."

Although mysterious, being human we crave the voice of solitude. In moments of great stress and indecision, we frequently turn to the muted company of nature—the forests, fields, streams, stars, the magnificence of sea and mountains. These ethereal encounters are not of long duration, for ultimately we must face the problem, answer the question, reach a decision, begin the journey.

Searching for solace, we turn to the creations of man —writings, paintings, discoveries. Even so, God's persistence will not permit us the luxury of aloofness too long. He wants us to hear the voice and feel the urgency that separates us from the lonely crowd. Like our Lord struggling in the wilderness to ascertain vocation, God's will and way for his life, so each of us must wrestle with self in the frightening wilderness of lonely silence.

It is encouraging to note that following Jesus' temptations "the devil left him, and behold, angels came and ministered to him" (Matt. 4:11, RSV). Our Lord's options and problems, however, were not allayed forever. Each day he was tormented, exposed, and accused. Even so, he used periods of aloneness to experience renewal. "After he had dismissed the crowds, he went up into the hills by himself to pray. When evening came, he was there alone" (Matt. 14:23, RSV).

There is a peculiar loneliness associated with evening.

It is always, or should be, a period of reflection and thanksgiving. It affords opportunity to rediscover the Christ of the hills and of human hearts.

The affection of the great chief justice John Marshall for his wife, Mary Ambler, who became a semi-invalid early in their marriage, approaches poetic perfection. Love for his wife grew with her declining years. Despite heavy responsibilities, including momentous court debates, he was exceedingly attentive and did everything possible to bring her joy and comfort.

The giant statesman with rustic manner and romantic feelings delighted in sharing with "Polly" insights and conversations from the outside world. She was Episcopalian; he, Unitarian. Even so, Justice Marshall would frequently come home after the service and read to his wife from the Book of Common Prayer, the Gospel, Collect, and prayers for the day.

There is an inconceivable company of shut-ins in varying degrees of infirmity who hunger for visitation, to hear the Gospel read and prayers offered. When have you visited one of these?

In his book *Survival Plus*, Reuel L. Howe challenges the reader to live inclusively for survival. Moreover, by living charismatically and openly, growth and joy are inevitable. Most of us live as exclusionists, commuting in and out of escape shelters, attitudes, habits, and prejudice, at will. Exclusionism, however, creates bitter, bigoted, bile-producing old age. "Changing from exclusionist to inclusionist," says Dr. Howe, "means changing from a life based on fear to a life based on trust; from being a closed person to being an open person; from being motivated by a sense of ought-ness to being a self-determining, deciding person; from being a controlling individual to becoming an interactive one who is willing to participate with others in relationships of trust." [2]

Being known, accepted, appreciated, involved in enjoyable employment fill the hours and the heart with hope. It is important to develop a diversity of interests, thus affording new, continuing opportunities for expression and experimentation. Basically, however, it seems to be a matter of rediscovering and reaffirming purpose, living for others, performing ministries in the community, demonstrating Christian faith. There is no place quite like the church to experience renewal and personal mission.

The church should afford fellowship, exhibit concern, and demonstrate love. No one should be lonely. "You shall love your neighbor as yourself" (Matt. 19:19, rsv). This is the directive for the Christian community; it must characterize its uniqueness.

Tread softly, speak gently whether to soldier, student, deserted husband, or bereaved wife, for loneliness is a harsh and relentless reality. The impressive executive and the hilarious entertainer may be lonely. High office, heavy responsibility, professional success tend to generate loneliness. Conquering it is far more complicated and difficult than overcoming some minor social impediment or fulfilling production quotas.

Loneliness is vast in its dimensions and varied in cause. Whether temporary or permanent separation, the nature of one's work, polarization of society, there are few experi-

2. Reuel L. Howe, *Survival Plus* (New York: Seabury Press, 1971), pp. 168–69.

ences comparable to that created by purposelessness, living incognito.

The late E. Stanley Jones wrote in *Victory Through Surrender* that for fifty years his home was a suitcase. He never knew loneliness because long ago he surrendered his life to Christ.

Travel, television, books, clubs, concerts, crowds may momentarily alleviate one's loneliness, but it returns. Only a genuine relationship with God creates at-homeness. As Dr. Jones stated, "Self-surrender not only takes away loneliness, it takes away fear of death. It takes away fear of death because you have already died, you have died to you as the center of you."

Solitude shadowed Jesus in his temptations, during early hours along the seashore. In Pilate's palace, Gethsemane, Golgotha, he was alone; yet God enabled him to overcome. The Galilean was frequently referred to as "a man of sorrows, and acquainted with grief" (Isa. 53:3, RSV). He gained strength from solitude. When the Lord desired to fortify himself for difficult undertakings, he chose to be alone. Jesus preferred private meditation to mass inspiration.

Whatever the nature of your loneliness, remember a host of mighty souls, treading life's highway, have preceded you. Remember, too, that you—through the discipline of prayer, persistence of faith—may have fellowship with God and his people. What was true of patriarchs, prophets, and Christians of yesterday can likewise be true for you. Everyone is lonely until he finds God.

4

The Syndrome of Suffering

Man is born to trouble as the sparks
fly upward.

Job 5:7, RSV

I picked up the book of Job today by
chance and found my own history there,
precisely.

George Bernard Shaw

Pain is man's friend, in its curious,
paradoxical way.

Karl Menninger

Suffering—even the most apparently
meaningless—can be used.

Earl A. Loomis, Jr.

In my opinion whatever we may have to
go through now is less than nothing
compared with the magnificent future
God has planned for us.

Romans 8:18, Phillips

The syndrome of suffering is not a theoretical conundrum. It is an inescapable fact. History reveals it; life substantiates it.

Why in the name of religion or humanity does God permit untold suffering? Conjure the pain from war, famine, floods, disease, earthquakes, exposure. Every perceptive soul hears the sounds of suffering and sadness.

A P–51 fighter crashed against a mudbank in South Korea. The catapulted pilot landed on his back forty feet from the flaming wreckage in a drainage ditch. His flight suit was on fire. At the base hospital doctors cut away his clothing and shuddered at what they saw. The left side of the lieutenant's head was severely burned; his face smashed; cheekbones and jawbones broken. Hands were burned; body broiled from waist to ankle. He also sustained compound fractures of the right leg. Although in a coma, he refused to die.

This flyer was only twenty-five years old. Two days after the accident he exclaimed, "I'm alive! I'm alive!" His battle for survival began March 21, 1952. The saga of his suffering reads like a modern version of Job. He underwent fifty-eight major operations in three years. Racked with pain, hooked on drugs, addicted to alcohol, he withstood discouragement and inconceivable torture.

Thirty-nine months after the crash he was discharged from the hospital and ordered to Langley Air Force Base, Virginia, for nonflying duty. With characteristic persistence the recuperating flyer persuaded a pilot to check him out in a T–33 jet trainer. Then he challenged colleagues to put him "through the wringer." He passed every test with flying colors!

66

The Syndrome of Suffering

Captain James Arthur Young was restored to unrestricted flying status in January 1956. In October of 1965 he volunteered for duty in Vietnam. Subsequently his squadron flew one hundred missions over Southeast Asia. On January 27, 1972, President Nixon nominated this phenomenal man to the rank of brigadier general. Subsequently he assumed the responsibilities of assistant deputy chief for the United States Pacific Air Forces. General Young is an indestructible monument to the human spirit!

Pride of the Yankees, Lou Gehrig, also knew how to live with pain. The latter years of his remarkable career are especially pertinent. It began in the winter of 1938–39. An excellent ice-skater, that season he fell repeatedly. The following spring at baseball camp he worked hard, but something was missing. The perfect player was no longer at first base.

On April 30, 1939, the Yankees played the Senators. Gehrig went to bat four times and struck out in order. The Yankees lost. Monday was an off day. Tuesday, before playing the Tigers, Lou told his manager, Joe McCarthy, in the dugout: "I always said that when I felt I couldn't help the team any more, I would take myself out of the lineup. I guess that time has come."

The Iron Man of baseball who played in 2,130 consecutive games went to the Mayo Clinic where x-rays revealed he had seventeen assorted fractures which had healed by themselves. Yet he had never missed a game! The tragic pronouncement, however, was that Lou was living on borrowed time. He had amytrophic lateral sclerosis which eventually took his life.

One of the most unusual ceremonies in the history of

baseball took place at Yankee Stadium, July 4, 1939. Celebrities from all walks of life gathered to salute this courageous gentleman. At last Gehrig stood before the microphone and, in a voice trembling with emotion, said, "For the past two weeks you have been reading about a bad break . . . yet, today, I consider myself the luckiest man on the face of the earth."

Many positions were offered Lou Gehrig, including thirty thousand dollars from a restaurant for use of his name. He accepted an appointment by Mayor LaGuardia as special parole officer to derelicts at six thousand dollars a year. Gehrig continued his efforts when he could no longer move his arms. He died June 2, 1941, with never a word of complaint!

Members of the older generation often speak of the softness of American youth, their lack of toughness and dedication. They should have known Diann Fox. As a freshman at the University of Iowa en route to dinner on October 6, 1967, she was involved in an automobile accident. This lovely coed sustained injuries which left her paralyzed from her shoulders down.

For seven long weeks Diann lay in University Hospital at Iowa City, Iowa. Then she was moved to Younker's Hospital, Des Moines. Because of her condition and inconceivable adjustments, doctors suggested a parent stay with her every night, a loving ritual faithfully performed.

Through the knowledge of science and medicine, skill and empathy of physicians and nurses, supporting love of family, Diann was eventually able to take therapy and manipulate an automated wheelchair. Despite her courage and care, she died May 15, 1969.

The Syndrome of Suffering

God gave Diann, but he did not take her away! Let us not blame the heavenly Father for such accidents. He does not violate laws of the universe to correct the judgment or carelessness of his children in a split second of decision. He does not wish anyone to be maimed, tortured, or killed but permits it. We are thankful for the Dianns who teach us patience and faith in suffering.

Life is expensive. It costs too much to be born, too much to live, and too much to die. In addition, many catastrophic diseases require astronomical amounts of attention, patience, and financial resources. Kidney dialysis, for instance, can cost twenty-five thousand dollars a year. Ten thousand Americans suffer from irreversible kidney failure annually. Recent supportive legislation will be most helpful. Even so, it is difficult to comprehend the anguish associated with the liquidation of one's assets, knowing all the while the loved one faces a premature death.

Consider the mental anguish of the twenty-seven passengers and crew of twin-jet DC 9, Southern Airways Flight 49, which in November of 1972 was commandeered over Alabama by three hi-jackers! During thirty hectic hours, the plane covered four thousand miles, three countries, stopped at eight cities, and made two trips to Cuba.

Fathom the helplessness of those aboard—the threat to dive the plane into Oak Ridge, Tennessee, the tires shot out, the hopelessness after takeoff from Orlando, and the crash landing in Havana.

Captain Bill Haas of La Grange, Tennessee, who was in command of the craft as a favor to another pilot, was the epitome of courage. A passenger reported "he instilled confidence." Co-pilot Billy Johnson sustained a shoulder wound, and several passengers were injured. Much of the time they were forced to ride in a crash position, leaning forward, head down. At one point the men were ordered to strip to their shorts for an hour. To those aboard the ill-fated flight and to relatives and friends, the hours were interminable. One passenger said, "It was hell!" How does one measure such anxiety, fear, suffering? How is it that some can rise to the occasion while others panic and still others give up? The raw courage and resilience of individuals is as miraculous as it is magnificent.

A different tolerance for emotional suffering is seen in the Eagleton affair. Beyond the bitterness and the obvious deficiencies in the democratic process of nominating a president and vice-president of the United States, Americans will long remember the 1972 campaign.

Early proliferation of Democratic candidates, winning of the nomination by Senator George McGovern, and the hurried selection of Missouri's junior senator, Tom Eagleton, dramatically illustrate political subterfuge and personal suffering. The *Wall Street Journal* hailed the selection of Eagleton as a "perfect nobody." Later it developed that Senator Eagleton bore unsuspected scars. His offense? He had been hospitalized for emotional fatigue and depression.

Although there is no stigma per se, nor should there be, attached to emotional disturbances and distress since one out of every ten Americans needs psychiatric help, it soon developed that Eagleton would not be acceptable. After days of astute readings from political barometers and many hassles, Senator Eagleton was dropped from the Democratic ticket.

The Syndrome of Suffering

Regardless of blame, archaic conclusions, political petti-fogging, think what this decision meant to Senator Eagleton and his family and friends! He endured unspeakable suffering and humiliation. His comportment throughout the ordeal was commendable.

Turning a chronic disability into an imaginative resource is an indication of character, a challenge to "basket cases" and hypochondriacs.

It is a miracle that Christy Brown lived. This lump of helpless humanity—one of twenty-two children, nine before him and twelve afterward—survived largely through the grace of God and the untiring, loving efforts of his mother who, despite a drunken bricklayer husband, saw something worth saving in her deformed child. Born with severe cerebral palsy that rendered him unable to walk, eat, or drink without assistance, Christy learned to read and write. He educated himself through works of his favorite author, Dickens, and has become a lyrical and provocative writer.

At age thirty-seven this handicapped Irishman produced a fantastic book. One is tremendously impressed by his vocabulary, choice of words, sentence structure, and descriptive powers. He is hailed as a literary genius. And to think he typed every letter of *Down All the Days* with one little toe!

Here is a sample of Christy Brown's word power: "God put women on this earth to suffer. That's what my Ma always said. She was right. That's all women can do—suffer. With their men and with their babies. Men are sometimes worse than babies. Twelve of us my Ma had by the time the eldest was twenty. She died last year giving birth to the last. A little boy. He lived, but he's all twisted and deformed. Can't talk or walk, can't feed or dress himself. Dribbles all the time. They say he's mental. They want to put him in a home. But I won't let them." [1]

This shockingly realistic story—the triumph of a human being over adversity—brings to mind Paul's counsel concerning human impediments. Every man lives with some handicap—physical, mental, moral, spiritual—but however fragile and painful we may feel, God can use imperfection to his glory. Here is Paul's admonition: "This priceless treasure we hold, so to speak, in a common earthenware jar—to show that the splendid power of it belongs to God and not to us. We are handicapped on all sides, but we are never frustrated; we are puzzled, but never in despair. We are persecuted, but we never have to stand it alone: we may be knocked down but we are never knocked out!" (2 Cor. 4:7-9, Phillips).

Athletes are not alone in their ability to break pain barriers. Many souls live in quiet desperation. Mrs. Janice Oakley, age thirty-four, Roberta, Georgia, was queen of the Crawford County Sesquicentennial, November, 1972. Prior to the historical pageant she sustained a broken rib. Despite pain and fever, she performed her duties. Four days later she died with double pneumonia.

This ill woman confided to a friend that she went through with it, not only because she was being honored, but also to register appreciation to the community for its thoughtfulness at the time of her husband's accidental death. The strength and sweetness of some individuals are inspiring.

---

1. Christy Brown, *Down All the Days* (New York: Stein and Day, 1970), pp. 196-97.

The Syndrome of Suffering

In the history of the Disciples of Christ in Illinois there is reference to a remarkable man by the name of John F. M. Parker who within one year's time lost a son, a daughter, his farm, and his wife. Despite such devastating losses he was able to say, "I know whom I have believed, and I am sure that he is able to guard until that Day what has been entrusted to me" (2 Tim. 1:12, RSV).

A radio announcer daily admonishes his listeners to "keep on keepin' on." To phrase the philosophy of perseverance another way, Rocky Marciano once said, "A champion must learn to bleed a little." Regardless of vocation, one must increase his tolerance for suffering and harassment.

A police station was bombed. Damage was estimated at one-quarter of a million dollars. Even more serious was the threat to human life, including that of a black judge who was in his office at the time of the explosion. A few nights later his home was burned. Since he was one of my favorite people, I telephoned, but I could not get through. When at last I reached his office, his secretary advised, "The judge is on the bench."

What courage! This is one meaning of "keep on keepin' on," "bleeding a little."

Analyzing certain British victories over the French, the Duke of Wellington said, "British soldiers are not braver than French soldiers; they are only brave five minutes longer." The Christian is not much stronger than the average person, just a little longer.

Although no one invites suffering, it may add new dimensions and unexpected qualities to life. One does not have to be a Picasso to appreciate shadows in a painting, nor a Bach or Beethoven to understand how turbulence adds

73

excitement and beauty to a score. Life without difficulties would be flabby and unchallenging.

Uncertainty, anxiety, and danger are synonymous with living. From Abraham obeying the demands of God, Rachel weeping for her children, to Madame Curie and her colleagues wrestling with the secrets of radium, knowing all the while they were jeopardizing their health, to Albert Schweitzer in the swamps of Africa, passion for adventure and service haunts and satisfies the human spirit. Man is forever rising from endurance to reverence.

Among Aldous Huxley's sophisticated dialogues in the scientific projections of *Brave New World*, Savage is afforded two alternatives—an insane life in a Utopia, or a sane life in a simple Indian village. One is stimulated to visualize a society without heroism, the cutting edges of pain and anxiety. It is "Christianity without tears," announced the Controller. To which Savage retorts, "But the tears are necessary." And so they are.

Katherine Mansfield declared, "I do not want to die without leaving a record of my belief that suffering can be overcome, for I believe it. Everything in life that we really accept undergoes a change. So suffering becomes love."

Inevitably we wonder why the good must suffer. Why is it that some people are accident prone, apparently have more than their share of problems?

In *The Sound of Music* the Reverend Mother asks Maria why she has come to the convent. Hesitatingly the distraught girl replies, "To discover and do the will of God."

What is the will of God?

A bright young man, graduate of Purdue University, active in church, happily married, was among the first

American fighter pilots in Vietnam. He has been missing for several years and was not one of the returning POW's.

A sweet child, victim of polio, will wear braces the rest of her life; a saint is immobilized with painful arthritis; a mother is dying of cancer; a father is struck down in the prime of life by a heart attack. Why such pain, suffering, and death? What do we mean when we say this is the will of God?

Some earnestly believe that convulsions of nature and personal tragedy are designed by God to accomplish his purpose. Others are equally convinced that life's mysteries and misfortunes are compounded by God to teach his children something they need to learn.

In moments of stress we are given to quote Scripture to substantiate situations. A few years ago when Dr. Helmut Thielicke endured a long illness, some friends tried to comfort him with the familiar words from Romans: "We know that in everything God works for good with those who love him, who are called according to his purpose" (8:28, RSV). Later, Thielicke said, "There is one thing I would say to these people. Nothing good happened to me in my affliction. It was not good."

Illness and misfortune do not please God. Healing, joy, love, and life are the will of God, not untimely death, affliction, and suffering. Christians need to be careful lest they leave the impression that goodness automatically emanates from evil; joy, from sadness; health, from illness.

Others maintain that God uses pain and bereavement to punish. Often I have heard distraught people cry out, "What have I done to deserve this? What has happened in my life that is so bad that God is punishing me?" Frequently I have replied, "Nothing, my dear!" The Book of Job should destroy the myth of punishment.

Some honestly believe God's will is achieved by causing people to die, thus bringing them to himself. God takes unto himself the faithful, but he does not inflict death in order to receive them. We hear it said, "God has taken my dear one," which is tantamount to saying God killed my love.

We learn very few lessons, I think, from being overwhelmed or highly perplexed. Let us be slow to assume that God imposes afflictions to teach us, for I believe the premise is wrong. God does not afflict anyone. We are stricken through neglect of the natural laws of health, disobedience, disease, catastrophe, sin, and accidents. Health is the will of God, not illness.

Fantastic theological systems have been woven around the controversy of the cross of Christ. It is good to ponder the mystery. Luther maintained that our thinking should begin at the wounds of Christ, but was it really the will of God that his Son should be harassed, brutally beaten, and nailed to a tree? Is our God brutal and sadistic? If so, is it any wonder that humanists, intellectuals, and critics reject this kind of God?

A God who measures x-number cubic centimeters of blood from his Son to atone for the sins of others does not impress me, but a God who permits such brutality and still blesses the murderers and the victim does affect me. A God who manipulates law and order to his advantage does not leave me in awe and admiration, but a God who forgives those who attempt it, does.

Why then do horrible things happen? Would it be helpful to suggest tragedies are statistically possible? Studies indicate that a given percentage of automobile drivers will have accidents; others will be sick, flunk out of school, become addicted to drugs. Exposure involves risk.

Creation is composed of many things that react in many ways. Germs and viruses are also parts of creation. A drug which heals one individual poisons another. When we catch cold or have poison ivy or athlete's foot, we do not cry out, "This is the will of God." Rather, we seek medical attention. If we are a helpless victim of another on the highway, we do not say, "This is the will of God." It is the behavior of man!

Horrible things happen because of human limitations and failures. Awful things occur because of our weaknesses and attitudes. Let us not confuse the frailties of men with the will of God.

The spiritual life is not axiomatic; it involves struggle, choice, and commitment. The Christian is not immune to mystery, pain, or misfortune. "Not a hair of your head will perish. By your endurance you will gain your lives" (Luke 21:18–19, RSV). What an encouraging thought. Life, not death, is the will of God!

Jesus declared, "My food is to do the will of him who sent me, and to accomplish his work" (John 4:34, RSV).

What did he do? He mingled with all kinds of people, with myriad problems, assuring them of the Father's love; he pinpointed sins of leaders and institutions; he preached and practiced reconciliation, mercy, and love. He lost himself in service, but his service record did not preclude physical, mental, and emotional pain!

Jesus accepted his mission as the will of God. His intuitiveness and perception enabled him to understand fully God's purpose for his life. Therefore, he could say, "For this is the will of my Father, that every one who sees the Son and believes in him should have eternal life; and I will raise him up at the last day" (John 6:40, RSV).

In *The Spiritual Legacy of John Foster Dulles,* Dr. Henry P. Van Dusen reminds us of Mr. Dulles' painful and lingering illness and how, during those days when suffering sharpened, the noble man derived comfort from listening to the great hymns of the church. His recordings included "The Spacious Firmament on High," "When Morning Gilds the Skies," "Work for the Night Is Coming," "All Praise to Thee, My God, This Night," "God of Our Life, through All the Circling Years," and "Through the Night of Doubt and Sorrow."

As the mortal body of John Foster Dulles was borne to its resting place in Arlington cemetery, it was altogether fitting that strains of the statesman's favorite hymn should greet his funeral cortege:

> Through the night of doubt and sorrow
>   Onward goes the pilgrim band,
> Singing songs of expectation,
>   Marching to the promised land.
> One the object of our journey,
>   One the faith which never tires,
> One the earnest looking forward,
>   One the hope our God inspires.

Whatever the circumstances, the Christian is to remain steady and confident. Because of his insistence upon truth, George Tyrrell of England was ultimately expelled from the Jesuit order and practically excommunicated from the Roman Catholic church. In the midst of his troubles he

78

wrote, "Again and again I have been tempted to give up the struggle, but always the figure of that strange man hanging on the cross sends me back to my task again."

Have we forgotten the tragedies that assailed Ralph Waldo Emerson? Poor health plagued him. After being ordained to preach, he came down with tuberculosis. Recovering, in 1829 he became pastor of Old North Church, Boston. That same year he was married. Two years later his wife died. A theological controversy cost him his pulpit. An observer wrote, "A doom seemed to hover over his family and his life but under the surface, dark as it was at the moment, a purpose was taking form in his mind. He knew he was born for victory." And so are we all!

The Christian answer to suffering, then, is not an explanation or a formula but the realization of a reinforcing presence, the awareness of Christ who comforts and encourages in heartbreaking moments. Peace often comes through pain. Frequently the frozen assets of suffering quietly shape one's faith, personality, and influence.

The Christian is not spared illness, pain, or death, but he is afforded the memory and ministry and promises of Jesus. Faith is trusting God with the outcome of our lives. Communing with him, we listen and gain strength; we follow and are not afraid.

John Greenleaf Whittier, the Quaker poet, summarized it beautifully:

> I know not where His islands lift
>   Their fronded palms in air;
> I only know I cannot drift
>   Beyond His love and care.

5

Are You Ready to Die?

Turn up the lights. I don't want to go
home in the dark.

O. Henry

Death wears a thousand faces but he is
always the same. Death is our destiny,
and death comes by disease, accident,
violence, or time. Death is nature at
work.

Carlyle Marney

You have not the faintest notion of what
it is to be eighty-five and three-
quarters dead.

George Bernard Shaw

Love is the infinite which is given to
the finite . . . Love, not help, is stronger than death.

Paul Tillich

I am the resurrection and the life; he
who believes in me, though he die, yet

81

shall he live, and whoever lives and
believes in me shall never die.

Jesus, John 11:25, RSV

Centuries before Jesus, Job asked, "If a man die, shall
he live again?" (Job 14:14, RSV).

Cicero journeyed to Necropolis, the city of the dead,
lighted a taper at the tomb of his daughter, and wept, "Is
this the quenching of thy life, O my daughter?"

When asked what he would do if this were his last
night on earth, John Wesley declared he would eat supper,
preach at candlelight, say his prayers, go to bed, and wake
up in glory!

After the *Titanic* had struck the iceberg and death
seemed imminent, John Jacob Astor and his valet, who
were among the passengers, changed into evening dress so
they might "die as gentlemen."

Men of every age have reflected on the mystery of death.
We are living in a day which attempts to dispel it. We
camouflage it; we deceive ourselves into believing that our
everyday existence continues forever. But in moments of
painful shock of perceptive insight we are brought face-to-
face with the reality of death.

There are two common attitudes toward death, either one
of which might well become a barrier to Christian faith.
The first is what many call the rational view, generally
appearing in two variations—the stoic and the existentialist.
Both agree that death is a natural conclusion of biological
existence; so make the most of it. But death is the end, says
the existentialist, the final absurdity playing havoc with

life. He believes the only meaning our lives have is the meaning we give them.

A different point of view is the philosophical or religious assertion. Even though man is destined to die physically, something in him continues. He is endowed with indestructibility.

Like the stoic and the existentialist, the New Testament regards death seriously. It is not something which happens to the body and leaves the soul untouched. Death affects the whole person. As Chester Pennington has said, "The opposite of everlasting life is not everlasting punishment, but death. Oblivion. Nothing. Just existing."

The message of Easter is life! It affirms that God is the Lord of life and those who commit themselves to him will not perish but live forever. God comes in Christ assuring us of his intention for preservation, yet reminding us of the part we must play in salvation.

To read Eugenia Price's *The Beloved Invader* is to be reminded that life has shocking ways of turning honeymoons into funerals. Ellen Gould died in the arms of Anson Dodge while honeymooning in India. The young minister and his charming wife had been guests at the home of a British precinct officer in Allahabad.

After eating some grapes, Ellen became desperately ill. All night Anson and Dr. Hayworth struggled to keep her alive. With the coming of dawn, she whispered, "Anson, don't leave . . . me." Her features changed. She was dead. In anguish the young minister cried. "No, God! No!"

The Right Reverend Edward Ralph Johnson, bishop of Calcutta, conducted the service of memory. Reflecting on the funeral, all the confused husband could recall was the paraphrasing of Jesus' words, ". . . though she were dead, yet shall she live."

It was a long, sad voyage from Allahabad to St. Simons Island, Georgia. During the weeks of heartbreaking travel, the young rector kept rehearsing Bishop Johnson's comment, "It is God's way not to waste anything. Even grief."

Friends at St. Simons shared the crushing sorrow. Memorial service over, Anson Dodge began the long, tedious, and challenging task of recasting his life. Like the Indian lover, Shah Jahan, who erected Taj Mahal, he, with the cooperation of his congregation, built a church in memory of Ellen—Christ's Church! This cruciform structure of white pine, paneled in cedar, with delicate stained-glass windows, not only memorializes the devotion of a people to Almighty God, but also the growing faith of their shepherd and his mature love for Ellen Dodge whose body was eventually laid to rest under its altar.

His grief is reminiscent of the bereavement of Naomi who, bereft of husband and sons, said, "I went away full, and the Lord has brought me back empty" (Ruth 1:21, RSV).

Death is frequently ravaging to a partner or relative. Not having been able to get beyond one's self to the reality, availability, and presence of God, the bereaved becomes a bundle of self-pity, a mirror of martyrdom.

In her penetrating book, *When You're a Widow*, Clarissa Start says one can surmount his grief. He can rejoin the human race, may even be a better member of it because of sorrow. She adds that one will eventually "sense a certain pity for those whose lives have not been touched by grief, for they have not lived life to the fullest."

Death is the inevitable experience shared with mankind. No one can die for another. Celebrities, saints and sinners, rich and poor, old and young, all experience death with us and we with them. Because of station and influence, few of us will receive recognition accorded a world citizen. Government buildings will not be closed when we die nor will the flag be flown at half-mast.

Death is the other end of life. To some it is restoration; to others, the answer to life's riddles. Some look upon it as sleep, a bridge from this world to the next. Others consider it the absolute end of all existence. Whatever your definition, death is the great democrat that reduces all of us to one denominator.

Like an ominous cloud, death hangs over us. We seldom talk about it; we are afraid. Though impossible, we attempt to escape its inevitability. The late William Randolph Hearst forbade anyone to use the word *death* in his presence; Philip II, king of Macedon, father of Alexander the Great, commissioned a servant to come into his presence daily and solemnly announce, "Remember, Philip, thou must die."

Death is inescapable. Without it there would be no room for birth; we could not be fully translated into the eternal. As Bishop Angus Dun put it, "Death measures the ultimate in courage and in love."

The poet-preacher of Scotland, George Macdonald, once remarked, "We die daily. Happy are those who daily come to life as well." It is everlastingly true that we die a little at a time through compromise, indulgence, indifference, deterioration, hardship, and sin.

There is an amazing and encouraging sentence in John's Gospel: "Truly, truly, I say to you, the hour is coming, and now is, when the dead will hear the voice of the Son of God, and those who hear will live" (John 5:25, RSV). John would have us remember Jesus dealt with all types of death and conquered them. The Easter gospel declares the dominion of death could not hold Jesus. That miracle destroyed its finality forever.

Death is an unscheduled adjournment in the agenda of life. Like a long, tedious meeting when the chairman, sensing the weariness of the group, announces intermission, so death comes. Unlike a prepared agenda, however, one has no notion how long his life meeting will last. To some the adjournment comes quickly; others live to write many pages, indeed volumes, and die at an advanced age. The poets, Keats and Shelley, died in their twenties while Picasso lived to be ninety-one.

Buddhism teaches that life is created and destroyed moment by moment; a new self is constantly emerging. So does Christianity! Throughout the journey, no person remains the same. Like frames in a motion picture, though changing, there is remarkable continuity.

Christ teaches that life is indestructible; love, eternal. Jesus declared and demonstrated that whether one lives or dies, he belongs to God. Even so, we become frightened at the thought of dying.

Some two million Americans die every year from an assortment of causes. In addition to normal and vocational deaths, more than fifty-six thousand Americans lose their lives in accidents annually. We are also witnessing shocking deaths and maimings resulting from privately owned firearms. Shootings in the United States aggregate twenty-one thousand people a year.

In 1971 guns figured in 10,500 murders, 80,000 injuries, and 220,000 robberies. Guns were used in 65 percent of homicides, 63 percent of robberies, and 24 percent of aggravated assaults.

There are some ninety million guns in civilian hands today. A new one is purchased every twenty-four seconds. Americans average 135 handguns per 1,000 people; Canada, 30 per 1,000; Israel, always in turmoil, has only 10; Finland, the Netherlands, Greece, Great Britain, and Switzerland have fewer than 5 handguns per 1,000 population.

Concerned citizens are asking, "Why can't something be done about all this shooting?" "Why should anyone, regardless of disposition, who has the money, be allowed to buy a handgun?" "Why aren't there more uniform and stringent gun regulations in the United States?" Ironically enough, Senator John Stennis, who voted against an earlier gun bill, was shot down in front of his home in the nation's capital.

We are a violent people. America, like most nations, was born in revolution. Each generation demonstrates the arrogance of power and the symbols of strength and determination. This image is perpetuated in language, toys we make and buy for children, sporting events we like, and TV shoot-outs.

As with other national problems, gun-control regulation is tied in with politics and lucrative economics. The strongest lobby for open season on guns is, of course, the National Rifle Association. With a membership of one million, purportedly capable of speaking for thirty million gun owners, it wields tremendous influence. This powerful organization can generate five hundred thousand letters to congressmen in a matter of seventy-two hours. Couple this power bloc with the manufacturers of firearms, the National Wildlife Federation, and other conservation groups that depend on hunting fees and licensing for income, plus those citizens who feel it necessary to keep firearms in their homes, and one begins to glimpse the dimensions of this Frankenstein.

Still another obstacle to safer gun controls is traceable to existing laws. In 1969 the Commission on Violence reported there "is a patchwork quilt of more than 20,000 laws, many of them obsolete, unenforced, and unenforceable." There is also the question of personal psyche. The psychiatric health of the purchaser is as important as the distribution and availability of weapons. Eventually and inevitably, public opinion will force Congress to pass some prohibitory laws. The present situation is intolerable. Meanwhile, let us not forget the moral law: "You shall not kill" (Exod. 20:13, RSV).

I was summoned to the hospital to see a patient who was depressed and uncommunicative. Meanwhile it was discovered she had swallowed an overdose of sleeping pills. The young woman became violently ill while we were talking. She clutched my hand as nurses and doctors pumped her stomach. After the ordeal, she calmly stated, "If I had succeeded, I would have destroyed the only distinctive thing God has ever given me."

"And what is that, my dear?" I asked.

"My life!"

Suicides are escalating. Whatever the motivation or definition, acceleration of this tragedy in our country and throughout the world suggests overwhelming difficulties many human beings face.

My first funeral service as a seminarian was for an elder in the student parish who took his life. I was frightened and frustrated. The counsel of one of my dear professors, H. H. Tweedy, continues to be clear and supportive: "Conduct the service as if he were a saint. God alone is judge."

The phenomenon of suicide is as old as human awareness.

Marilyn Monroe was found dead in her bedroom Sunday, August 5, 1962, apparent victim of an overdose of sleeping pills. During agonizing moments when she struggled with the decision—whether to give in to what Freud called "the death instinct" or to live—she died reaching for the telephone. However suicide occurs, it is a belated and dramatic cry for help.

There is a beautiful page in the Monroe memoirs. It is testimony to the lingering love of one of her husbands, Joe DiMaggio, who has red roses delivered to her resting place three times a week.

Anthropologists affirm that primitives practiced self-destruction. This form of death is found in annals of the Egyptians, Hebrews, Romans, and Greeks. Many Christians took their lives—or permitted themselves to be killed —during the reign of Caesar Augustus. By the fourth century, however, St. Augustine vigorously opposed suicide on the grounds that it precluded repentance and violated the Sixth Commandment. Later Thomas Aquinas argued that self-annihilation was an indication of immaturity. Moreover, he felt the act was detrimental to the Christian community as it usurped God's power to dispose of man at his discretion.

Emile Durkheim classifies suicide as egoistic, altruistic, or anomic. It can involve the range of human emotions from exaggerated individualism to an exaggerated sense of personal importance. Whatever the cause, there are from twenty-seven thousand to thirty thousand Americans who take their lives annually. This represents eighty deaths a day! On a world scale there are about one thousand suicides every twenty-four hours. Despite ambiguities associated with suicide statistics, it is estimated there are four to five million persons in the world who attempt self-annihilation every year. This is a sad commentary on modern civilization.

Two hundred suicide prevention centers are scattered across the United States. Manned by teams of professional and lay people committed to listening, they serve and salvage depressed and desperate individuals. Church members should be among the first to detect, react, and respond to potential suicide victims.

In 1735 John Wesley embarked as a missionary to convert Indians of Georgia. It was a perilous journey lasting four months. He was attracted to a group of Moravian exiles on shipboard. One day as these brave souls were assembled in worship, a severe storm broke and waves lashed the sailing vessel. The mainsail was ripped to shreds, windows in the cabin smashed; water covered most of the ship. Terror echoed in the raging winds!

The Moravians continued their worship. Wesley was amazed. Later he asked if they had been afraid. The leader replied, "I thank God, no!"

"And what about the women and children?"

"Couldn't you see they were not afraid?" he answered. "When God is with us there is nothing to fear, not even death."

The young crusader returned to his journal and wrote, "I have a sin of fear." And so do we all.

When Mills B. Lane, Jr., fifty-nine, president of Citizens and Southern Bank, Atlanta, announced retirement plans, he shared a profound philosophy, "My daddy told me that business, like trees, start dying from the top . . . so I am getting out of here to make way for fresh, young blood." His successor, Richard Leigh Kattell, was thirty-five years old.

Mr. Lane's reference to his father's observation brings to mind a line from Shakespeare's *Macbeth*: "I have lived long enough; my way of life is fall'n into the sear, the yellow leaf." A wise man knows when to quit. The Peter Principle is so much in evidence, it is refreshing to hear an able executive call for a younger man to assume the load.

It is sad to see once useful public servants, reluctantly facing retirement, hanging on to establish some tenure record or to qualify for a larger pension. Change is inevitable; it is a sign of life. Without change there is stagnation, death. Even so, one must face the unpredictabilities of his departure.

The last words of the great English novelist and historian H. G. Wells were, "Don't bother me, can't you see I am busy dying?" We all are. It is a matter of how readily we recognize and accept the process.

There is a remarkable headstone in the cemetery of Christ Church, Frederica, Georgia. A marble hall depicting the globe stands about four feet high. Written in circular fashion near the top of the sphere are these words: "Lois Mary McClain, born 11 May, 1930, married 29 December, 1956, died 25 July, 1960. The greatest maxim I can give is make the most of the hours you live."

When is one dead? Some time ago Professor Michael Shaara of Florida State University survived a massive heart attack. When stricken, he was teaching a full load, producing educational television shows, and writing a book. Furthermore, he was smoking three packages of cigarettes and consuming twenty cups of coffee a day. Fortunately for Dr. Shaara, heart specialists were immediately available upon his arrival at the hospital. The patient was clinically dead. He had no pulse; he was not breathing. After fifty-five minutes of cardiac massage, electroshocks, use of drugs, a miracle occurred—he was alive!

One day in the summer of 1967 Jackie Bayne of the 196th Light Brigade was on routine patrol with his dog, Bruno, when the animal stepped on a mine. Shrapnel tore into the GI's legs. By the time the young soldier arrived at the field hospital, doctors found no pulse, no breathing, no audible heartbeat. After a considerable lapse of time, physicians pronounced Bayne dead. For several hours thereafter he lay at a grave registration unit. Then a medic cut into the soldier's groin to insert embalming fluid. A faint pulse was detected, and Bayne was rushed back to the medical center where eventually he revived. Later he was flown to Walter Reed Hospital. Army doctors refer to the case as a "rarity."

When it was announced that President Calvin Coolidge was dead, it is reported Dorothy Parker, short-story writer and poetess, quipped, "How can you tell?"

The Karen Anne Quinlin case reemphasizes the necessity for a definition of death. It has concerned physicians for years. Now it is concerning theologians, moralists, lawmakers, judges, journalists, and many others. Following the historic and successful heart transplant by Dr. Christiaan N. Barnard and his surgical team in Cape Town, South Africa, the December 18, 1967, issue of *Newsweek* said: "Doctors can now play God. They can alter the genes, build artificial parts of the body . . . they can even transplant the human heart—the symbol of life itself—from one body to another!"

Until recently the moment of death was thought to be the instant the heart stopped beating. Advanced knowledge indicates one is dead when his brain is dead. We know it is possible for one to be legally dead for years and return; it is also possible to be spiritually dead, wholly insensitive to truth and injustice, and be converted. No one is dead until God passes judgment.

Like life, death is nontransferable. Whether considered traumatic, tragic, a blessing, or a contest between the will to live and the desire to return to inorganic matter, death poses a sincere problem for most, if not all, human beings. How do we handle it?

Like birth, puberty, and marriage, death is a most

significant occurrence, not only for the individual, but also for society. As with most profound events, death deserves ritual and ceremony. It is a rite of passage from this world to the next. As Shakespeare said in *Henry IV*, ". . . we owe God a death." It may be postponed but never canceled.

The late Dag Hammarskjöld declared, "In the last analysis it is our concept of death which decides our answer to all the questions that life puts to us."

In her inciteful book *On Death and Dying*, Elisabeth Kübler-Ross, M.D., shares observations from clinical studies made with students of the Chicago Theological Seminary on two hundred dying patients. They agreed the most fearful crisis in life is dying. How does one face death?

As would be expected in a society of computerized choices, the mass man, cosmetic woman, both patient and public, are carefully protected from the trauma of death. Professional chores in the hospital are so carefully calibrated that the patient is frequently unaware of his condition and has few, if any, options. He must take what comes and hope for the best, all of which heightens his fear of death.

Added to the strangeness of the environment and sterility of professional conversation, the terminally ill patient is often left to fret and fight loneliness and fear with the minimum of consultation, comfort, or assurance. It could be that the psychology of sophisticated Americans in preventing their children from witnessing death may unintentionally create an ambivalence toward death that will levy heavy penalties in the future.

Dr. Kübler-Ross and her associates confirm observations

of many, namely, there are visible stages through which the dying person normally passes. Following the shock of learning one is really living on borrowed time, the patient may attempt to deny the pronouncement and seek isolation. This is a rather natural reaction. It may even be reflected in other members of the family.

As a rule, however, this stage does not prevail too long and is likely to be followed by a period of anger, "Why me?" Resentment may escalate into harsh threats and accusations. Usually the gentle therapy of conversation and love enables the failing person to become less caustic.

A prominent third stage is bargaining. "If God has decided to remove me from the earth, has paid no attention to my demands and questions, perhaps he will listen if I am more polite . . . if I promise to do better . . . will give . . ." While in this sober mood, one may make commitments and promises if in turn God will prolong life. This, of course, is a postponement tactic, designed to gain time for good behavior.

However, when the fatally ill individual can no longer deny his plight and must face painful surgery again and again, he may become severely depressed. In fact, both the patient and his loved ones may assume this posture when impending loss is taken into full account.

If there is genuine understanding and loving support, the dying person often emerges from depression, gradually assuming an attitude of acceptance. This is not altogether a happy stage, but it is one of rational acknowledgment and preparation for the journey. Conversations are less strained, little things become more important, and reminiscing enjoyable, attention to business inevitable, and writing and reviewing the will imperative. Clearing up misunderstandings and reconfirming one's faith also become matters of urgency. But this can be a time of great and permanent satisfaction, one of penitence, courage, and commitment.

Regardless of the circuitous path, the loved one—or you!—may have traveled, there come shining moments: the confirmation of life, the persistence of hope. However complex, painful, mysterious life has been, now there is purpose and victory. One is certain that man is as much a part—and more—of the universe as the moon, stars, sun, trees, and sea, that the loving Creator preserves his own; nothing is lost.

The approach of death underscores the swiftness, precariousness, and preciousness of life. It makes us aware of our limited sojourn and of the greatness of the eternal now. Life everlasting begins, not with the moment of death, but with the amount of spiritual birth.

When George Papashvily was a small boy in the Caucasus, Russia, he was taken to visit a revered old man who lived in the mountains. It was customary for each child to take the hermit a gift in return for which the little one received a proverb.

Although frightened, George timidly approached the stern-looking sage. The wise man asked the youngster what he wanted and where he wanted to go when he grew up. After exchanging questions, the centenarian whispered in the lad's ear, "This minute, too, is part of eternity." The truth, of course, eluded the boy for years, but later he realized, as do we all, that birth and death are not irreconcilable parts but form a harmonious whole.

Eternal life is not limited to the future; it is a degree

of existence which begins in the eternal now and continues forever. The gospel teaches that life is to be considered in terms of quality, not longevity; life is not an endless existence but a marvelous relationship with God and his children. To see death as the continuation of God's love should help still our fears and generate peace and faith in the perpetuity of personality.

Our emotional adjustment and acceptance of Christ's victory over death provides a context for confession and courage. Being finite, nothing completely removes all doubts and fears. Relationship to the living Christ is the quintessence of assurance, the essence of hope.

Show Me the Way to Go Home is Red Barber's spiritual autobiography, a pilgrimage of faith. This noted sports announcer of a few years ago shares his anger with God for taking his mother when she was quite young. Red was so resentful that he stayed away from church ten years. Eventually, through touch-and-go experiences with his wife who lost two babies and almost the third, he came to himself. Ultimately he obtained the distinction of becoming a lay leader in the Episcopal church. He still is.

Red Barber's father was an engineer on the railroad in North Carolina, a good man, quiet, who became increasingly stolid after his wife's homegoing. When death was imminent, none of the relatives could remember if the old man had ever been baptized. Deafness made conversation difficult. With his father sitting up in a chair and all but oblivious to what was going on, after the custom of the Episcopal church, Red baptized his father.

The next day, to everyone's astonishment, senior Barber raised his head and stuttered, "I want to see a preacher."

Being in a Baptist home, they sent for a Baptist pastor who read and prayed. Afterwards the young minister took the old man's hand for a moment. William Lanier Barber looked him in the eye and with steady voice said, "All my life I have loved God Almighty. That will have to be enough for me now."

Red Barber declares it was the most beautiful, complete confession of a man's faith he had ever witnessed.

Later that afternoon Mr. Barber said three things to his son. "Walter, I want you to have my watch; you are the only one in the family with any sense of time."

Then he said, "Walter, I love you."

His final admonition: "Walter, go on back to your job."

How human can you get? How Christian can you become? The essence of being yourself is when you are yourself before God! Before your family! Before death!

If death is the consummation of visible life, the commencement of new spiritual living, then it behooves one to prepare for the adventure. Unfortunately death's shadow is so frightening that relatively few give this exodus the attention it deserves. Many families are at a total loss when death invades the circle.

How well I remember my mother's homegoing. This remarkable Christian, who lived every day of her life and who constantly referred to the inevitability of death, left a written memorandum of her wishes. It named the mortician, ministers she desired, hymns to be used, pallbearers—the entire memorial service thoughtfully, carefully planned. It was our solemn responsibility to implement her wishes. How much easier it would be if all of us could be so considerate and precise.

Are You Ready to Die?

The last words of dying people are intriguing. They project philosophies and provide biographies.

Actor Howard Lindsay said to his actress wife, "It has been a wonderful journey. And I've had a wonderful companion. And I've enjoyed every minute of it."

Julius Hobson has probably done as much as any other American to advance positive changes in human relations. A bright, aggressive, relentless worker, he is dying with multiple myeolma. Hammered by pain, he is completing a book on black Americans.

He faces death rather arrogantly and unrepentingly: "I don't feel guilty for a god damn thing I have done on earth. I believe it was Thoreau who said, 'What demon possessed me that I behaved so well?' "

Listen to St. Paul's valedictory: "I have fought the good fight, I have finished the race, I have kept the faith. Henceforth there is laid up for me the crown of righteousness, which the Lord, the righteous judge, will award to me on that Day, and not only to me but also to all who have loved his appearing" (2 Tim. 4:7–8, RSV).

The Christian sees life as a struggle and death as a transition from the visible to the invisible world. The monumental confidence of Jesus ever looms before us: "Father, into thy hands I commit my spirit!" (Luke 23:46, RSV).

Early believers saw in Jesus the miracle and magnificence of life. They saw in him God's gift, a Savior, one who conquered death and gave new dimensions to life. His declaration encouraged and strengthened them: "You must not let yourselves be distressed—you must hold on to your faith in God and to your faith in me. There are many rooms in my Father's House. If there were not, should I have told you that I am going away to prepare a place for you? It is true that I am going away to prepare a place for you, but it is just as true that I am coming again to welcome you into my own home, so that you may be where I am" (John 14:1–5, Phillips).

Therefore, to early Christians and to us the resurrection is more than an isolated incident in the mystery of Christ. It is not an addendum attached to the gospel story, not a Hollywood version of a psychologically appropriate ending, but part and parcel of the entire life and message of Jesus. The issue is not the survival of personality beyond death. The issue is the resurrection of Jesus Christ!

The reality of the resurrection converted the early disciples and placed Jesus in a new perspective. The power of the resurrection brought the church into existence and produced the New Testament.

The power of the resurrection changed calendars, schedules, and spirit of institutions. It caused early Christians to observe the Lord's Supper as a means of expressing their gratitude for God's gift and for the opportunity of sharing his presence.

The power of the resurrection gave man a new perspective, a new source of reality, confidence, companionship. Early Christians believed that in the crucifixion and resurrection of Jesus, God demonstrated his limitless love and his indestructible power.

There is a lovely conversation in *Papa's Daughter*. Button Franzon knew that papa had not been afraid of death. She remembered that once when they had first come to America the whole family had taken a trip to Niagara Falls. She was young then, but she had never forgotten papa's words. He had held her arm as they walked along admiring the wonder of God's creation, the magnificently beautiful falls.

As they stood and listened to the mighty roar of the gigantic waterfall, the old man declared it reminded him of the rushing, unpreventable approach of death. Although we are thrown, tossed, and bruised by its rapids, life suddenly moves on, sweeping us into the stillness of the lake below. "Death," said Pontus Franzon, "is a tunnel between heaven and earth."

Cane Ridge Meeting House near Paris, Kentucky, is a historic place—the scene of great and moving revivals in the nineteenth century. There Barton W. Stone and four other Presbyterian preachers organized the Springfield Presbytery in 1803. On June 28, 1804, "The Last Will and Testament" was formulated. Eight items were "willed." The first, "That this body die, be dissolved and sink into union with the Body of Christ at large."

In the cemetery of this old church are some fascinating headstones. Among them:

> Here lies Nathaniel Rogers who was born in 1755.
> He was a member of the convention that formed
> the constitution of Kentucky in 1799. But what is
> of far more consequence, he was a member of the
> church of Christ in the bosom of which he died.

Death is a horizon; a horizon is but the limitation of one's sight.

In *For You Departed, a Memoir*, Alan Paton of South Africa shares the intimacies of married life, love, grief, loneliness, and death. With the transcendence and tenderness of a poet, he expresses his feelings for Dorrie Francis, his wife. Written in the first poem, this love story shimmers with understanding, courage, and Christian faith.

Shortly after their marriage July 2, 1928, it was discovered that Mrs. Paton had anoxia of the brain, an insufficient oxygen supply which resulted in difficult breathing, at times necessitating oxygen feedings.

Delicately the gifted writer recaptures in conversational style highlights from their thirty-nine years of marriage. He speaks of her grace in suffering, moments of worship, bedside communion, and at last her homegoing in October, 1967.

His reference to the funeral in St. Agnes Church, Natal, the spray of St. Joseph lilies cut from their own garden, the hymns, prayers, the archbishop's statement, "the church itself packed with people of all nations under our sun," beautifully describes Christian triumph and community. The service concluded with the stirring hymn, "Now Thank We All Our God."

After the benediction, Paton joined his sons, David and Jonathon and the reader, Murray, in carrying the casket from the church to the hearse. What a profile of tenderness and strength, love and courage, constancy and faith! In Paton's description of Dorrie's increasing illness, confinement, hypostatic pneumonia, one does not find a trace of bitterness or cowardliness, only graciousness and love.

> Sleep well, my love.
>> Give rest, O Christ, to thy servant with thy saints: where sorrow and pain are no more, neither sighing, but life everlasting. Thou only art immortal, the Creator and Maker of man:

and we are mortal formed of the earth, and unto earth shall we return: for so thou didst ordain when thou createdest me, saying, Dust thou art, and unto dust shalt thou return. All we go down to the dust; and weeping o'er the grave, we make our song, alleluya, alleluya.

Give rest, O Christ, to thy servant with thy saints: where sorrow and pain are no more, neither sighing, but life everlasting.

* * * * * * * *

So do I weep over the grave, and make my song, alleluya, alleluya, alleluya.[1]

Long shall I remember my father's death. He lived seventy-five miles up country from the church we were serving in Richmond, Virginia. He had been ill for a number of months. Though the Sunday sermon had not been rewritten, I obeyed an inner voice and made the journey home.

As I arrived, the nurse told me father had hoped I would come. She cleared the room, and we had a wonderful visit. Death was imminent, but he was calm and lucid. He gave me several business directives and then told me he would soon be going. I thanked him for all he had meant to me, and in deep sorrow I said, "Give my love to mother!"

Instantly he replied with all the animation his weakened condition would allow, saying he visited with her the night before and she was awaiting his arrival. I kissed him good-by. As I turned to leave, he said: "Curt, I'll see you in the morning!"

This I believe. This is my faith!

---

1. Alan Paton, *For You Departed, a Memoir* (New York: Charles Scribner's, 1969), p. 20.

Epilogue

Montui Vivos Docent
(The Dead Teach the Living)

Although this Latin motto is frequently found in pathology laboratories and morgues, we are slow to grasp its inescapable message. Medical science has greatly increased life expectancy, particularly in the Western world. Since 1900, America's percentage of population above sixty-five has about tripled. But has it greatly increased life commitment?

Despite medical progress, the mortality rate remains at precisely 100 percent. No one escapes death. The Christian, of all people, should live, not only to change concepts of death, but to fulfill the mission of Christ. Jesus came to give life, not just things, an abundant, beautiful life-style and ministry.

Andrew Carnegie, son of an immigrant, ultimately a successful manufacturer and phenomenal philanthropist, desperately desired additional years. He believed if he could live another decade he might make a lasting contribution. He offered two hundred million dollars for another ten years. This is $54,794 a day; $38, a minute. No one could accommodate him!

Life is never available to the highest bidder. It belongs to God. Although beyond the realm of bargaining, life can be used to assure its continuance. The secret is to initial with one's witness what will outlive self.

HOW COME WE'RE ALIVE?

Woodrow Wilson declared he would rather fail in a cause that would someday succeed than to succeed in a cause which would ultimately fail. In this perspective of delicate differentiation in values the Christian is challenged to live all the days of his life.

Horace Mann was such a gentleman. Obsessed with the dream of public school education, he struggled against difficult and embarrassing odds. This well-educated, disciplined man frequently found his guiding star unnoticed by critical and complacent contemporaries. When the state board of education was formed in Massachusetts, he was named secretary, a position he accepted at considerable financial sacrifice.

In 1853 Horace Mann was elected first president of Antioch College where he also taught theology and philosophy, remaining until his death in 1856. Meanwhile he demonstrated the practicality of coeducation and succeeded in raising academic standards. In his final baccalaureate address at Antioch, the distinguished educator recounted for the students his lifelong ambitions and struggles, declaring he could wish for another warfare on behalf of right. Dramatically he exclaimed, "Be ashamed to die until you have won some victory for humanity."

Life is far more than chemical recycling; it is a witness to the highest and best that we know. God challenges his children to be a blessing, to implement his will in a computerized society that is far more interested in precise calibration of things than in compassion, more concerned with income than eternity.

"This is eternal life, that they know thee the only true

God, and Jesus Christ whom thou hast sent" (John 17:3, RSV). The translation of this declaration into daily mission is the secret of contagious living. To live forever is to comprehend the dimensions of the moment; to discover purposeful involvement; to meet every decision, problem, opportunity with intelligent persistence and dedicated effort. The way one manages his affairs, the integrity and courage with which he performs, characterizes his philosophy of life.

To live forever is to demonstrate faith in God, in the human race, and in one's self. To live forever is to demonstrate hope in the most discouraging of times, knowing that hope is an imperishable possession. To live forever is to demonstrate love. Love is eternal.

Life is a gift from God which he alone can guarantee. The way we meet it, our consideration for others, the scope of our interests, the depth and joy of our stewardship indicate our gratitude and our relationship to Christ.

A Christian is not only perceptive but generous. While he can take with him on the ultimate journey only faith, hope, and love, he can distribute visible possessions, tangible, measureable things, in such a way that his faith is augmented and his homegoing less traumatic.

In five, fifteen, twenty years from now you may be dead. Even so, death affords an opportunity to participate in the ongoing drama of life.

Beyond vocational skills or personal services, an increasing number of people feel impelled to bequeath their bodies to medical science when they die. You—and you alone—have the right to redistribute your terrestrial packaging. This can be accomplished through an anatomical bequest. Whatever your particular interest in physical existence, it can now be augmented by donating portions of your body to help sick people get well, or your entire body to further medical research and education.

The Uniform Anatomical Gift Act, introduced in 1968, was adopted by all fifty states in 1971. There are those whose theology will not permit them to participate in such a physical reservoir of helpfulness. Should you share this conviction, there is no criticism. To those who have no qualms about contributing their bodies to others, there are helpful and reassuring stipulations. The most obvious feature of the Anatomical Act is, of course, the individual delegates posthumous rights—not surviving kin. Anyone who dies without specific burial instructions leaves the disposition of his body to relatives and friends.

Another important feature of the act is that the donor agrees that his death must be determined by a doctor who is not involved in transplants. Furthermore, if it develops that one's organs are not acceptable, then the donee (hospital, clinic, medical school, or patient) has the right of refusal. The Uniform Anatomical Gift Act was designed to simplify the donation of parts of the human body to assure proper procedures, safeguards, and dignity.

Among the many sources for Uniform donor cards are: Continental Association, 59 East Van Buren Street, Chicago, Illinois 60605; Medic Alert, Yurlock, California 95380; National Kidney Foundation, 116 East 27th Street, New York, N.Y. 10016.

Others believe that by permitting their bodies to be

frozen, at some future time science may discover ways of restoring life.

A significant way to perpetuate influence is to invest your financial resources in the future. The Tax Reform Act of 1969 has made impractical the creation of a personal foundation unless assets are in the tens of millions. It is much more practical to establish a memorial endowment fund at your church, college, or university which will be managed in perpetuity by the institution.

A Christian should make a will. What is a will? It is your most important legal document. It is not so much the itemization of your assets as the articulation of your faith. To die without a will is to die without having the last word over that which you have earned, inherited, or with which you are entrusted.

Studies reveal that less than 50 percent of American adults have properly drawn wills. Usually there are three kinds: nuncupative (oral), holographic (handwritten), and the statutory, frequently called the English will. While it is your prerogative to make determinations, in a day of specialization and proliferation of laws, you need one with expertise to assist you—an attorney.

If you do not make a will, you deny yourself the privilege of presiding over your estate. Furthermore, if you do not make a will, a third party—the state—makes it for you and distributes possessions according to law, not necessarily in agreement with your desires. The result may be financial snares, exorbitant taxes and fees, family squabbles, lawsuits, and a general dissipation of funds.

Many prominent people do not make wills. Peter

Marshall, the eminent and persuasive preacher, is said to have left no will. Pablo Picasso, the most influential and prolific artist of the twentieth century, did not leave a will. Strange notions and poor logic are associated with drafting bequests; to some it is to sign a death warrant. Fear of death prevents intelligent participation in the future.

Further down the spectrum are those who live as though they were never going to die. Therefore, they postpone making a will; half of them leave nothing to the church.

Another common tragedy is the man who neglects to update an early will, causing distribution to be based on family situation, charitable interests of many years earlier, and a much smaller estate.

Some feel that writing a will is so personal that to broach the subject is to commit an unpardonable sin. Others leave the impression that they do not care what happens to institutions or individuals after they are gone.

Still others assume a will is for the well-to-do. As we have indicated, it is a record of a man's faith, not an ostentatious display of wealth. Although a legal instrument for the distribution of one's property, it is also one's legal resurrection, by which he is privileged to speak after death.

Not everyone is as fortunate as Alfred Nobel who in 1888 read his own obituary in a French newspaper. One of his brothers died. A careless reporter used a statement prepared for the wrong man. Alfred, principal inventor of dynamite, was disappointed with the published account. He was described as a "merchant of death" who had made a fortune from explosives and human exploitation. This haunting image caused him to reevaluate his life and revamp his will. Subsequently, he provided for the now famous Nobel Peace Prizes.

Not every will is Christian. Some are the epitome of selfishness. Others are sarcastic, strange, and complex. A man left forty thousand dollars to a cat. An eccentric woman left even more to an animal hospital with the stipulation that these words appear over the entrance: "The more I saw of people, the more I thought of dogs."

A will is Christian when it reflects one's genuine commitment to Jesus Christ. A Christian acknowledges God's ownership and gratefully assumes the role of trustee.

James Barrie wrote a play entitled *The Will*. The drama opens with an idealistic young couple in conference with an attorney. They are newlyweds. Philip Ross, the husband, had inherited a sum of money and wanted to make certain his wife would receive it in case of death. The young wife, also unselfish, insisted that Philip leave some of the money to his cousins. The lawyer was impressed. "You are a ridiculous couple, but don't change."

Quickly the drama moves into the future. Twenty years pass. The couple returns to the legal firm for counsel. Their estate is sizeable. The Rosses have lost their original concern and compassion. She wants to be sure her husband does nothing foolish; the cousins should not be remembered in their wills. Interest in a convalescent home has waned. There is considerable debate and controversy.

Years pass. At age sixty-five Philip Ross returns to the same law firm to discuss his estate. Meanwhile his wife has died. His children, he claims, are unworthy. Relatives and community projects are deleted; no mention of the church. Dramatically he dictates to his lawyer: "I leave . . . I

leave . . . My God, I don't know what to do with it!"
As he paces back and forth before the attorney, he stops
and shouts, "Here are the names of half a dozen men I
fought to get my money. I beat them. Leave it to them
with my curses."

A Christian does not leave his money with curses but with
love.

Elizabeth Yates' book, *Amos Fortune, Free Man*, thrills
me. It is the saga of a man born in Africa and sold into
slavery, July, 1725, in Boston. The Quaker family
surrounded him with affection and understanding. When
the Copelands died, Amos was sold to the Woburns of
New Hampshire, where he finally gained his freedom May
9, 1769.

Amos Fortune, a good man who worked hard, sustained
the loss of two wives, and at age eighty became a land-
owner. Knowing his days were numbered, he had many
conversations with the Lord concerning his stewardship.
Finally he went to see Deacon Spofford about drawing
his will. The black man declared he loved two institutions—
the church and the school. From his little bag Amos
drew out one hundred dollars to purchase a silver communion service for the church. Although he and his
family were members of the local congregation, wor-
shiped regularly, they were relegated to the gallery. Then
he unwrapped a handkerchief containing two hundred
forty-three dollars. This he designated for the school
which had allowed his stepdaughter to attend.

There was a resurgence of strength, pride, and confidence
as Amos walked home. He had demonstrated a continuing

stewardship; he had confirmed his faith; he had been better to others than others had been to him. Looking skyward, he said to the Lord, "You can come any time now for I'm ready." What a contagious Christian!

Do not underestimate God's power to multiply gifts made in genuine love. The smallest bequest can and often has inspired the stewardship of a congregation. To a Christian the writing of his will should be the climax of a contagious witness; it should name and provide, not only for one's family, but also for institutions dedicated to Christian nurture.

Is it important to your life that the Christian message has been preserved and communicated by each previous generation? How do you assess your obligations to posterity? The Christian steward is not distinguished by the accumulation of his possessions but by the way he uses and distributes his resources. Writing a Christian will should not be an isolated, secret experience. Churchmen could learn from extremely wealthy families who discuss openly their estates before finalizing bequests. Such a practice not only has creative possibilities, builds family loyalty, but also minimizes future conflicts.

After itemizing all possessions, noting persons and institutions to be remembered—including names and addresses —designate the amount or percentage each beneficiary is to receive. A listing of liabilities is also essential to intelligent future planning. Writing a will is a technical task. A lawyer is needed. His counsel is invaluable.

Name an able executor who then chooses the probate attorney. Some have paid dearly for wills drawn by friends of the deceased who, in turn, also served as executor of the estate. It is not at all necessary to have the same person. In fact, the advantages are quite the opposite. Incompetence can be exceedingly expensive. If an executor is not named, the court will appoint an administrator.

The executor is charged with a variety of responsibilities, including choosing the probate attorney, inventorying assets, paying just debts, and establishing a trustee account to receive all monies during the probate process. This individual arranges for the estate to be appraised. He is obligated to file and pay federal, state, and inheritance taxes. Giving an itemized account of his stewardship to all concerned is likewise required of the executor. He must also see that the will is legally implemented, distributions made, as well as the transfer of all properties and securities.

The first step in the probate process is reading the last will and testament. If agreement is reached that the instrument is the most recent and valid, the executor named should then be duly appointed. To avoid any misunderstandings and conflicts, destroy all copies of old wills when a new one is written. Place copies of the last will and testament in an unquestionably secure place (a lockbox at the bank), and notify the executor of its location.

We are rapidly approaching the place in our economy when the church can no more fulfill its mission on the receipts of a given generation than can a college, university, or library.

How well I remember a' man who attended church but was inclined to be sensitive and critical; he was not known for generosity. In fact, some men hesitated to call on him for his annual pledge. In their eyes he was not doing enough for the church; yet when he died he left an interesting will. After the life-use by his widow, his estate of more than five hundred thousand dollars went to his church. No one suspected such commitment.

Another memorable gentleman was a businessman whose wife taught in our church school. Following her sudden death, he talked with me about an appropriate memorial. I mentioned a number of possibilities. He was not interested. This all transpired just prior to my leaving the country for several weeks. It was agreed we would resume conversations after vacation.

Upon returning home, I found my friend in the hospital ill, inarticulate. He died. Reviewing conversations, I wondered if we had really communicated. To my surprise, he left his entire estate of approximately two hundred thousand dollars to our church with no strings attached. And to think, this man was not a member!

A faithful woman died. She had lived comfortably but inostentatiously. In her will she designated ten thousand dollars to her church. Apparently this dear soul was a tither as the estate was one hundred thousand dollars.

That venerable and vivacious gentleman from Alabama, Justice Hugo Black, was as unique and provocative in death as in life. Being a remarkable student of the United States Constitution, he traveled with a small edition in his pocket. Following Mr. Black's death and in accordance with his wishes, friends who came to the mortuary to pay their respects saw this distinguished American lying in an unfinished, plain pine casket. Moreover, every visitor signing the guest book received a pocket-sized copy of the Constitution.

Associated with one's homegoing should be something which suggests his life and witness.

A perceptive business executive said to me, "Have you ever noticed how few people remember the church in their wills?" This is a sad commentary on Protestantism. Many good stewards terminate their trusteeship with death.

In one large, prestigious church during our ministry the pastors buried 135 people, some of them extremely wealthy. Yet to my knowledge, only fourteen left that church any of their possessions.

No one is ready to die until he has made his last will and testament. It does not assure eternal life, but it does register faith in the future.

Glossary of Legal Terms

Administrator: A person appointed by the court to administer the estate of an intestate decedent where there is no will, no executor named, or where the named executor cannot or will not serve. This person has limited authority. Among his duties are those of collecting assets of the estate, paying debts, and distributing residue to those entitled.

Administratrix: A woman who administers the estate of an intestate decedent.

Ancestor: One who has preceded another in a direct line of descent; a deceased person from whom another has inherited.

Ancillary Administration: When a decedent leaves property in a foreign state other than the state of his domicile, administration may be granted in such foreign state for the purpose of collecting assets, paying debts, and bringing the residuary to the general administration.

Beneficiary: Every trust must have a beneficiary; individuals included must be identified. The person who receives property, income, or other assets by will is called the beneficiary.

Bequest: A gift by will of personal property.

Charitable Deductions: Certain specific contributions to charitable institutions are allowable under the law. Such gifts may not exceed a designated percentage of one's income or one's estate. When properly made, charitable gifts are nontaxable.

Codicil: A testamentary disposition subsequent to a will, by which the will is altered, explained, added to, subtracted from or confirmed by way of republication, but in no case totally revoked. A codicil is an addition or supplement to a will. It must be executed with the same formality as a will, and when admitted to probate, forms a part of the will.

Competent: One is declared competent if he has the mental capacity to comprehend the nature of the situation, the act in which he is engaged, understands relationships under the law and the consequences of his decisions.

Conservator: A person appointed by probate court, having given bond, to have custody and control, according to law, of the property of a ward or one who has been found incapable of managing his affairs.

Contemplation of Death: As it relates to federal estate taxes and gift taxes there is a presumption that the transfer, if made within three years of the date of the donor's death, is presumed to be in contemplation of death to avoid estate taxes unless the presumption can be overcome by showing that life motives controlled.

Devise: A testamentary disposition of realty; a gift of real property by the last will and testament of donor.

118

Domicile: That place where one has his true, fixed, and permanent home; principal establishment, to which, whenever one is absent, he intends to return.

Donee: One who receives a gift.

Donor: One who makes a gift or creates a trust.

Dower: The provision which the law makes for a surviving widow from assets of the husband's estate for her support and nurture of their children.

Estate: The property, real and personal, of a decedent. An estate comprehends everything one owns, although the form of said property may change from time to time.

Estate Planning: The process whereby a person plans the arrangement, management, and transmission of his assets so that he and the object of his bounty may derive the maximum benefits therefrom during his lifetime and after his death.

Estate Tax: An estate is a separate taxable entity from the decedent and comes into existence with the death of the decedent. With the exception of deductions and certain credits, the estate of a deceased person is usually computed on the same basis as for other individuals.

Executor: An executor is the person named by a decedent in his will to administer his estate, making distribution of properties as directed. If the person so named is a woman, the title is executrix. The executor is the personal representative of the deceased having authority from him to carry his will into effect.

Fiduciary: A person holding the character of a trustee or a character analogous to that of a trustee, in respect to the trust and confidence involved in it and the scrupulous good faith and candor for which it requires.

Gift Tax: A tax levied upon the right to make a gift during one's lifetime.

Grantor: A person who creates a trust.

Guardian: One lawfully invested with the power and charged with the duty of taking care of a person, managing the property and rights of another who, for some peculiarity of status, defect of age, understanding, or self-control, is considered incapable of administering his own affairs.

Half Blood: Refers to the relationship that exists between persons who have same mother or father, but do not have the second parent in common.

Heir: A person who succeeds, by the rules of law, to an estate of real and personal property upon the death of his ancestor, by descent and right of relationship.

Joint Tenancy: Ownership by two or more persons. Upon the death of a joint tenant, the remaining tenants take the share of the deceased. Finally, the last surviving joint tenant takes the property as a holder in severalty.

Inheritance Tax: A tax levied upon one who has received an inheritance.

Inter Vivos Trust: A trust which comes into being during the life of a grantor.

Intestate: A person is said to die intestate when he dies without making a will or dies without leaving instructions as to his wishes with respect to disposal of property after death.

Legacy: A gift of personal property by a will. It is sometimes called a bequest.

Marital Deduction in Federal Estate Tax: The federal estate tax is imposed on the taxable estate which is defined as the gross estate minus all deductions, fees, expenses, and the specific exemption of $60,000. Care should be taken to assure legal qualifications are met. The total marital deduction may not exceed one-half of the amount of the adjusted gross estate.

Power of Appointment: A power or an authority conferred by one person by deed or will upon another called the donee; to select and nominate the person or persons who are to receive and enjoy an estate or income therefrom or from a fund after the testator's death or the donee's death or after the termination of an existing right or interest.

Probate: A general term used to include all matters over which probate courts have jurisdiction; the judicial determination of the validity of a will.

Property: The rights and interests which one has in anything subject to ownership, whether it be moveable or immoveable, tangible or intangible.

Personal Property: Includes all property that is not real property.

Power of Trustee: Those powers expressly given to one qualified under duty to carry out the trust according to its terms or those the court construes as being given by the settlor. A trustee is obliged to defend the trust when disputed in court. He cannot attack its validity.

Real Property: The rights and interests of indeterminate or unfixed duration that one has in land and things closely pertaining to land. Technically it is an interest in things real.

Residue: That portion of an estate that remains after all charges, debts, distributions, and bequests have been satisfied.

Revival: Revalidating a will that has been revoked is called revival. Normally this can be accomplished by executing a codicil or the direct procedure of reexecuting the will.

Revoked: When the testator destroys, burns, deletes, or

otherwise defaces the drawn will with the intention of revoking it in whole or in part, it is invalid. One may also invalidate the original will by drawing another which is inconsistent with the terms of the first, or by disposing of the property to which the will related.

Testacy: The state or condition of leaving a will at one's death.

Testamentary Trust: A trust which will come into being after the death of the grantor.

Testate: One who has made a will.

Testator: One who leaves a will or testament in force at his death.

Trust: A right of property, real or personal, held by one party for the benefit of another, or an obligation arising out of a confidence reposed in the trustee, or representative who has the legal title to the property conveyed to him, that he will faithfully apply the property according to the confidence reposed, the wishes of the grantor of the trust.

Trustee: A person who accepts the obligation to perform according to the terms of a trust.

Widow's Allowances: When need exists and by court order or decree the estate is required to pay the widow or other dependents of the deceased a support allowance during the period of administration.

Will: The legal expression or declaration of a person regarding the disposition of his property after death; a written instrument executed within the formalities of law. There are normally three classifications: the holographic will (handwritten and signed by the testator himself); joint or mutual will (two persons with reciprocal provisions); nuncupative or oral will (declared or dictated by the testator in his last illness). Usually any person of legal age is eligible to make a will. For it to be valid, however, there are certain requirements: mental competency, intention, and legal formality. In some states witnesses are required.

Witness: Attestation of a fact or event; one who is asked to be present at the confirmation of an agreement that requires observation, testimony, or the affixing of signature.